PROSPECTS FOR IMMORTALITY
A Sensible Search for Life After Death

J. Robert Adams

Death, Value and Meaning Series
Series Editor: John D. Morgan

Routledge
Taylor & Francis Group
LONDON AND NEW YORK

First published 2003 by Baywood Publishing Company, Inc.

2 Park Square, Milton Park, Abingdon, Oxon OX14 4RN
605 Third Avenue, New York, NY 10017

Routledge is an imprint of the Taylor & Francis Group, an informa business

First issued in paperback 2021

Publisher's Note

The publisher has gone to great lengths to ensure the quality of this reprint but points out that some imperfections in the original copies may be apparent.

Library of Congress Catalog Number: 2002071726

Library of Congress Cataloging-in-Publication Data

Adams, J. Robert.
Prospects for immortality : a sensible search for life after death / J. Robert Adams.
p. cm. -- (Death, value, and meaning series)
Includes bibliographical references and index.
ISBN 0-89503-228-7 (cloth)
1. Immortality (Philosophy) 2. Consciousness. I. Title. II. Series.
BD421 .A33 2002
129- -dc21

2002071726

ISBN 13: 978-0-89503-228-7 (hbk)
ISBN 13: 978-0-415-78512-9 (pbk)

Dedicated to
ALEXANDRA

Table of Contents

CHAPTER 1

A Bird's-eye View

When you pick up a new book, how can you know if you're going to like it? You may be browsing in a bookstore, or a friend may have recommended a certain book to you and lent you a copy. Should you bother with this book? Will it amuse you? Will it teach you anything? Will it bore you? Is it a good story that will relax you? Will it make you think? I'll try to give you some honest answers about the particular book you are holding.

Amusement? I doubt it. The book is about death, and there are not a whole lot of laughs there. Most people are inclined to find death a bit scary. In this book, I will try to make it a little less so by analyzing death and its consequences.

New ideas? Yes, I think so. A glance at the bibliography should let you know because these are the subjects we look at. Science is more knowledgeable about the universe than it was not long ago, and I will try to give you some fresh ideas on the role we human beings play in it.

A bore? That depends. If you like to wonder about life, then you'll have some fun with the topics in this book. Our environment is mostly mystery, and mystery can be exciting.

A good story? No. It is not a story at all. It is my effort to put ideas on the table about life after death. Some of my ideas you will not have heard before. You will agree, or disagree, or come up with alternatives. You will think, if you don't mind.

In the present chapter, it is my intention to let you know what the book is about. You'll know where we're headed and not waste your time with stuff that doesn't interest you.

Before giving you a chapter run down, may I mention a brief word on the subject of bereavement? The loss of a loved one, as we know well enough, inevitably causes great sorrow, stress, and occasionally desperation for those that are left behind. For example (to get personal), when my Aunt Dorothy died and they lowered her body into a hole, I thought: "How can I go on without Aunt Dorothy? I have always had her friendship, her love, her wisdom. My life will be a bleak landscape without Aunt Dorothy."

You'll notice that, in thinking these things to myself, I was lamenting my own personal troubles rather than any problems Aunt Dorothy herself might be having as a result of her new status. We all do that. When we lose someone close, we may feel as though we've lost part of ourselves. But what about the departed person? What about the one, say Aunt Dorothy, that's been lowered into the hole? How is she making out?

That's exactly what this book is about. It's about the prospect that our existence is not simply snuffed out with our body. It's about the fate beyond death of the departed one. If you'd rather not think about life's end, then I guess this book is not for you. On the other hand, if you are curious about the possibility of an afterlife, then you may be thoroughly intrigued by what's coming up.

Now, let's get to the chapters.

UPCOMING CHAPTERS

We begin chapter 2 with the prediction that consciousness really does survive death. We suggest that Aunt Dorothy, even as we speak, is fully conscious. How could this be? Her bones are rotting in our local cemetery. Never mind. I propose a mechanism by which God does not abandon the dead but, on the contrary, preserves their consciousness for as long as the Universe lasts, and beyond. You can read about this in chapter 2.

After that, we move to chapter 3 and meet the Grim Reaper himself. We watch the Reaper plying his dark trade, taking away life and giving it back again. We look at temporary death, time of death, transplantation of organs, fear of death, and suspension of death by freezing.

In chapter 4, we ask: Can the Grim Reaper be held at bay? The answer is, yes. For how long? Indefinitely. How? By halting the aging process, use of stem cells, nanobots, freezing, gene splicing, even the fantasy of space travel. We speak about the necessity of death, and being overwhelmed by what has been called gray goo [1, p. 9] if there is no death.

In chapter 5, we talk about escape from death in terms of nerve impulses, electromagnetism, and quantum mechanics. If you hate technical stuff, this is the chapter to skip.

Chapter 6 examines existence by addressing questions posed by the late philosopher, Soren Kierkegaard.

The questions are: Where am I? Who am I? How did I come to be here? What is this thing called the world? How did I come into the world? Why was I not consulted? Where is the manager? [2, p. 267].

In chapter 7, we start tackling Kierkegaard's questions. We look at the origin of life on Earth, how it exploded into forms ranging from worms to people after living as single cells for three billion years. We examine the role of DNA in this explosion. We contrast the "what" of us (body) with the "who" of us (consciousness).

Chapter 8 looks at Kierkegaard's questions, "Where am I, What is this thing called the world?" We have a great time with soap-bubble universes, the birth and fate of our own universe, the ordinary stars as they change into red giants, white dwarfs, neutron stars, and black holes. We note the recent discovery that these heavenly objects appear to be moving away from each other at accelerating speeds in this crazy quilt-work of violence, this boiling cauldron of activity that we are used to thinking of as our peaceful sky. We observe that this same space is, according to my hypothesis, the home of my late Aunt Dorothy's consciousness, which is presumed to be alive and well.

Finally, we come to God, the supernatural controlling power over our lives. Kierkegaard asks, "Why was I not consulted? Where is the manager?" Kierkegaard seems to be looking for God, but can't find evidence for Him. He accepts God on faith. In this chapter, we take a look at how the followers of today's five major religions differ in their beliefs about God and about life after death. We compare these points of view with that of the Author's Saved Consciousness Hypothesis as presented in chapters 2 and 5.

Chapter 10 pokes fun at an imaginary meeting between Kierkegaard and the Author. We talk about the subjects covered in this book and about other things in life while the waitress keeps our tankards filled.

It should be made clear to the reader that the Saved Consciousness Hypothesis is guesswork. I will be perfectly frank about that. However, guesswork built on facts can have a useful place. If you can make a series of educated guesses and prove some of them right, you are building yourself a theory—a theory being a model of nature from which predictions can be made. It all starts with some sort of untested speculation, elegantly called a hypothesis.

I believe my hypothesis could provide some people with the rational hope of post-mortem existence. The hypothesis is not intended to offend, in any way, those traditional believers whose faith in an afterlife is based on spiritual reasons alone. This book merely provides a way of looking at the same subject in a non-spiritual way, namely, in terms of natural laws, the scientifically established laws of physics that we are familiar with.

There has been no work up to now, to my knowledge, directed at testing any part of the Saved Consciousness Hypothesis. And yet, at the rate that science is advancing, we should know soon enough whether this hypothesis holds promise. A hypothesis, if it does nothing else, often points the way to future research.

And now, if you are willing, please jump in with me and have a bit of fun in a search for life after death.

REFERENCES

1. B. Joy, *Why the Future Doesn't Need Us,* Wired 8.04, April 2000.
2. C. Wilson, *Afterlife,* Doubleday, New York, 1987.

CHAPTER 2

Personal Survival After Death

When the Authorities gave us a body, they made it wet and squishy. They constructed it from blood and guts that we learn soon enough don't last forever. When the blood stops flowing, our consciousness blanks out and the sense we have of ourselves is returned to zero. If the blood stoppage is permanent, it remains at zero.

"Nonsense," say the Hindus, Muslims, and Christians. "The soul is immortal, it doesn't quit, it goes on through eternity."

THE SAVED CONSCIOUSNESS HYPOTHESIS

In this chapter, I do not deal with questions of the soul. I leave them, wisely I think, to philosophers, theologians, and others who study God. Instead, I deal with the more science-related subject of memory and consciousness. My Saved Consciousness Hypothesis says these are potentially immortal. Specifically, it states:

1. There is a theoretical possibility during life of deploying and preserving memory and consciousness from the brain to some location independent of the brain.
2. This independent location is in subatomic space.
3. The memory patterns and flow of consciousness are being automatically recorded at this subatomic location continuously from birth to death, available for reactivation after death.

Now, you are not expected to swallow and digest these three statements at a glance. They will take some further explanation and reflection. They predict that there is a possibility for life after death. We will now explore the facts upon which these three statements are based.

The Case for Life After Death

Let's look at death. The world we know and are familiar with is a world in which death is final. Someone or something dies, and that's the end of it. When we die, the only evidence of our former life is: 1) a decaying corpse, 2) the recollections of those that remember us, 3) the changes we made to the world when we were alive, and 4) the DNA that we have given our children. As far as we can be certain, there is no other sign of us that is left behind. There is no credible indication that the life that was before is now any more. The fat lady, as they say, has sung.

What do we think of this? We don't like it. Death frightens most of us. In order to duck the prospect of death, we take refuge in speculation. Some of us speculate that the soul leaves the body and survives somewhere, somehow, in some nebulous state such as the Heaven or Hell we read about in the scriptures. Since the details of that world are not made clear to us, we can imagine anything we want, good or bad. The better we make our imagined picture look, the less are we bothered by the specter of death. So, we continue to speculate.

Now, what if our imagined afterlife was based on a few facts? I am suggesting physical facts that can be seen in this world. For example, I would like to see something that would indicate that my late Aunt Dorothy might still exist in spite of the death of her frail body. That is what the three elements of my hypothesis are all about. My hypothesis attempts to show how it is possible to anticipate personal existence after death based on what we already know about this universe.

We will now get out a magnifying glass and look at some facts. We will first look at memory. A search for Aunt Dorothy, I believe, can start at no better place than the memory circuits in her brain.

Saved Memory

> If immortality is what you crave, then you are much better off with the conception of yourself as fundamentally defined by information, rather than as a sort of immutable mind pearl, or soul of some sort [1].

Let us begin our inquiry into memory and death by asking this question: What are we talking about when we speak of surviving death? What could possibly survive? What do we want to survive? I believe the candidate for survival is the awareness one has of oneself as an individual person. We'll call it the Self. This is what we wish to avoid losing and it is an instinctive wish, programmed in our genes.

Now, this candidate for survival (the Self) depends on memory and consciousness for its existence. The Self is an ongoing thing built up from the events we experience every moment of our lives strung together like beads on a necklace. The Self consists of a whole necklace of connected memories. Wipe the memory banks clean, and the sense of self must be built up again from scratch. If you buy this, then here is the logical conclusion: if the Self as we know it is going to survive death, so must memory and the consciousness of that memory.

Having said this, where are we? We are looking for ways that Aunt Dorothy might survive death that are dependent on her memory and consciousness. We have postulated that, if she is to survive, then her memories and consciousness must survive. But now we are faced with an obvious question. How could memory and consciousness survive her dead and rotting body without involving spooks and violating the laws of nature? Well, first, let's take a closer look at memory with our magnifying glass and try to see what it's all about.

Memory is not just a black box localized at one brain spot. On the contrary, it is a widespread system made up of billions of nerves and their trillions of connections extending *throughout* the brain [2, 3]. The connections, called synapses, permit electrical impulses to jump from one nerve to another in a coordinated way. This network of nerves and their connections is what stores information such as the color of your dog's nose. We call it memory. The nose color is remembered when the same nerves and synapses are fired again that were fired when the image of the nose was first placed in the brain. Those networks were first fired when you looked at the dog's nose. They are fired again when you call up your memory of the dog's nose. Our memory is therefore a physical thing (nerve networks) from which information can be retrieved when certain nerves are re-fired or, as we might say, the right buttons in the brain are pushed. The late celebrated neurosurgeon, Wilder Penfield, was one of the first to press these buttons when he electrically stimulated particular areas of his patients' brains to bring forth specific memories.

Now let's take a big jump. Because memory is a physical pattern of nerves with their connections, it is theoretically possible to transfer this *pattern* (not the nerves themselves) from the brain to a point outside the brain. A principle of information theory states that any physical pattern can be duplicated at another spot in space [4, 5].

So now where are we? What does all this mean? It means that the *information* pattern in the brain representing memory does not have to remain in the nerve networks of the brain but can be transferred to another place that has nothing to do with the brain. Although this has never been done, it is theoretically possible to do it. The idea is crucial to the Saved Consciousness Hypothesis, because if memory can be moved to, and preserved at, a place independent of the brain, then this is a step toward the immortality of memory and consciousness. If you don't need the brain to support memory and consciousness, then memory and consciousness need not die with the brain. They can, in other words, wing it on their own!

This may seem preposterous, for there is absolutely no knowledge at present of how this transfer might be done, or whether or not it is automatically taking place, as my hypothesis proposes, without any help from us. We know that we need the brain in order to have memory and consciousness during life. The Saved Consciousness Hypothesis proposes that this memory and consciousness is transferable to a location independent of the brain and, in fact, that this is being done automatically without us being aware of it.

It sounds ridiculous, but consider. It is a fact that very complex information can be transmitted to another place by electronic means and preserved there as a duplicate. This is done, as you know, billions of times a day with modern communications technology. We are doing it every time we record a TV program on a videocassette or on a disk. Now, my hypothesis is stating that this transfer has been done with the information in your brain, in my brain, and in Aunt Dorothy's brain. Is Aunt Dorothy still out there somewhere, even though we know her brain is decomposing in the ground and returning to the dust from which it came?

In an attempt to answer this question, let's see what's involved when information gets electronically shifted from one place to another. For example, what goes on when an antenna radiates your favorite recording of Beethoven, Beatles, or Brookmeyer from New York out into space? You are taking a complex pattern of magnetic information that exists on a tape or disk in, say, New York City, changing the information to voltage fluctuations in a wire, radiating these fluctuations (which we neither see nor hear) through the vacuum of space to, say, the Moon. Okay. Now, suppose you are on the Moon and have a cassette recorder with you. You can start it up and recapture those voltage fluctuations to produce an exact duplicate of the original music [6]. You now have the same music on the Moon that you had on Earth. Play it, listen to it, dance to it. You have preserved a duplicate of the original.

Today, this transfer of complex information is routine. It doesn't impress us at all. A century or two ago, it could scarcely have been imagined. Now here is the big question that concerns us here: could similar magic be done with the information in the brain? Could brain information such as memory and consciousness be transferred from the brain to another place and be recaptured there without destroying the brain? Why not? If so, then we are on our way to immortality. Let's look further at what is happening when we transfer complex information on our own planet as a daily routine.

We see a whole range of information, not just music, moved from one place and replicated in a new place (or places) every day. It is so common we don't even think about it. For example, this transfer happens whenever we are watching television or a movie, telephoning someone, or operating a computer, scanner, printer, or camera. We are shifting and manipulating information, transferring it to another place, and replicating it there. And, as I have said, we now take this for granted. No big deal.

Do you see what this may imply? I am suggesting that your immortality is possible because any information, including the pattern of the memory grid in your brain, can theoretically be moved from point A to point B and be retrieved there. Just like a recorded version of Beethoven's fifth symphony, it doesn't matter if your brain is dead provided that the information in it has already been moved to a secure and accessible site. Your memory patterns and your consciousness of them are simply established at another site.

"Ah, but," you may object, "this is all very well for picture and sound which we know can be easily relocated. The brain is another matter, my friend. The brain's information is far too complex to be moved around and recorded elsewhere."

Not so. Theoretically, transmission and duplication can apply to any pattern of information, even the memory patterns of the brain. The entire memory in the brain, say at location A, can conceivably be transmitted and stored again at any other location, say B, without moving the brain. For example, Norbert Wiener [4], who coined the term cybernetics, correctly pointed out back in 1950 that, in theory, a whole human body can be transmitted by telegraph ("Beam me up, Scotty"). The Saved Consciousness Hypothesis does not go as far as Wiener, however, because it restricts transmission only to the memory patterns and consciousness wave that exist in the brain. It does not predict the relocation of the brain itself or of the body that contains it.

Now, what does this all mean to you and me? Simply this. If the translocation of the patterns of memory and consciousness is being done automatically during our lives by some unseen hand without us even knowing about it, then brain death and tissue decomposition need have no more effect upon the preservation of our self than would the destruction of a single recorded disk when a duplicate exists elsewhere. If it is granted that memory and consciousness give us our sense of self, and if it is found that they are transferable, then "we" are transferable without breaking any physical law.

We have now looked at the first element of the Saved Consciousness Hypothesis, which proposes that biological memory and consciousness patterns are transferable. But there are two other elements that must be added to this hypothesis if we are to make Aunt Dorothy immortal. They have to do with place and time.

The Subatomic Quantum World

Where, oh where, has Aunt Dorothy gone? If she exists, where is she? Element number two of the Saved Consciousness Hypothesis, which we are now about to investigate, deals with this question. Element number two states that she is in subatomic space. In other words, Aunt Dorothy's ongoing memory and consciousness exist in regions of space that are smaller than an atom.

Where, smaller than an atom? Where do these regions of subatomic space exist? The answer is: everywhere. Subatomic space exists wherever space exists. But we would like to know the coordinates of the small region of space where Aunt Dorothy's particular subatomic hell or heaven exists. We want to know where it is compared to something else in the universe.

Aunt Dorothy was a church-goer and probably thought of Heaven as a place or state outside and separate from our own universe of stars. But why outside the universe? Why not inside? And if inside, where inside? Is she in subatomic space within that galaxy of blue stars we see with our telescope millions of light years away? Or in that red tulip that blossomed yesterday in our garden?

As far as the Saved Consciousness Hypothesis is concerned, she could be living in either place as long as it is in a region of space much, much smaller than the point of a pin.

Why so small? Let's talk about size.

What we see around us we call *macro*scopic. We don't need a microscope to see it, so we can refer to this as the macroscopic world. It ranges in size from bugs to stars. When we want to look at smaller things such as bacteria or blood cells, we of course need a microscope. What we see in the microscope may be named a *micro*scopic world. The objects existing there can't be seen with the naked eye.

Now, if we ratchet down the size of things a bit more, say to the magnitude of a virus particle, then we need a special microscope called an electron microscope to see it. This new domain we may call the *ultra*microscopic world [7]. But, as small as this is, we are not yet in Aunt Dorothy's world. The ultramicroscopic world is still too big for her.

Is it possible to go down to a level where things are still smaller? Is there a tinier world than this for us to enter? You bet. There's another very interesting world but it's too small for us to make out through any microscope. It is a world smaller than a single atom. It is the world of subatomic space that is governed by physical laws very different from the laws we are familiar with in the world of large objects. What are these laws, then, that are so different than the ones we encounter in our daily lives, but which might support Aunt Dorothy's memory and consciousness after death?

The laws that control the way things happen in subatomic space are called the laws of quantum mechanics. This subatomic world with unusual rules is where my hypothesis suggests Aunt Dorothy may be leading a new life, and it is one of the strangest worlds you might imagine.

For example, quantum mechanics permits two contradictory statements to be true at the same time (she is 4 feet tall and she is also 12 feet tall). Ridiculous, but experimentally proven. Furthermore, quantum mechanics acts in many more than the four dimensions we are familiar with—probably at least eleven. It insists that light is both a wave and a particle simultaneously ("wave/particle duality"), and also that a force originating at a point A can be transmitted at once, with no time lapse, to act upon an object at another point B, even though the two points A and B are at opposite sides of the Universe. Zero traveling time. This transmission is called "non-locality communication." As outrageous as these strange discoveries in quantum mechanics may appear to be, countless experiments prove them right [8, 9]. These are the unfamiliar laws that Aunt Dorothy may have met when she departed this life.

The great minds that discovered and worked with this new physics (quantum mechanics) early in the twentieth century were baffled at what they found. Albert Einstein, one of the initial pioneers, said in a famous quotation that if quantum mechanics is right, then the world is crazy. Niels Bohr (the first person to describe the atom in terms of quanta) used to say that if you aren't confused by quantum physics, then you haven't really understood it. Richard Feynmann, a pioneer in quantum electrodynamics (some of us saw him on television network news explaining the explosion of the space-shuttle Colombia), said simply that *nobody* understood quantum mechanics.

And yet, as put by science-philosopher David Albert, quantum mechanics is the most precise mechanism for predicting the outcome of experiments on physical systems ever devised. No exception to its principles has ever been discovered, and nobody expects any [8, 9]. These are the rules that govern what happens in subatomic space.

If we were to ask a physics professor to tell us about quantum mechanics and its strange laws, we might get a discourse on superpositions, other universes, wave functions, wave-particle duality, indeterminacy, uncertainty principles, and other strange things. But mostly we'd get mathematical equations [10]. These equations are not everybody's cup of tea. Some of the equations, for example, have to do with "string" theory which implies that all the forces of nature (such as gravity) come from vibrations of tiny rips (strings) in space-time that are much smaller even than an atom [11]. Physicists are not all agreed on this. String theory is an active field of research today.

Does this have anything to do with Aunt Dorothy? Yes. It is this weird quantum world with its multiple dimensions and bizarre effects that the author suggests may serve as a possible home for the memory and consciousness patterns of Aunt Dorothy and, of course, the rest of us.

What about storage space? Would there be enough room in quantum space for the memory patterns of the countless dead? The answer is yes, more than enough [12, p. 40]. Physicist Freeman Dyson notes that quantum space has virtually unlimited capacity for information storage. So Aunt Dorothy would not find it crowded there. She would not have to elbow her way around.

If we wanted to locate Aunt Dorothy and ask her how she's doing, where in quantum space should we look?

As we noted earlier, quantum space fills the whole universe, existing wherever space exists. Since atoms are mostly space, it exists inside atoms as well as outside of them. One small region of this space, say the size of an atom, could probably hold the downsized memory patterns of all the beings that ever lived in this world with plenty of room to spare. The memories of the dead could be in the quantum space within us, between us, and all around us out to the most distant star. The Saved Consciousness Hypothesis predicts that the dead exist anywhere and everywhere in space. Exactly how and in what form will be investigated in chapter 5. There are a few other things that you may want to look at before we get there.

So, let's crank up our imaginations a bit more. If we are not convinced that my late Aunt Dorothy is in the quantum space of our own universe, then we might want to consider other universes such as those proposed by cosmologists Andrei Linde [13] and Hugh Everett.

Linde, for example, postulates that our universe (the one we see with our telescopes) is only one of a large system of universes. He visualizes them as bubbles that expand and contract in cycles. He proposes that each universe, including ours, eventually squeezes down in a Big Crunch to what is called a singularity that has effectively no size at all. The extraordinarily high temperature and density existing at such a point is too great to be imagined. At the singularity, says Linde, "all irregularities tend to get smoothed out." If so, then obviously information (such as our saved memory and consciousness patterns) would get smoothed out also and become lost. That would spell trouble for our immortality.

If the universe were to collapse in this way, would that be the end of our post-mortem selves? Would the Big Crunch not smooth all translocated memory and consciousness patterns out of existence?

Not necessarily. Not, that is, if we can credit some current theories. It is possible to imagine ways by which information might avoid being crunched out of existence by a universe that was squeezed down to a virtual point. For example, some say that space-time, though it appears smooth, has a foam-like sub-microscopic structure containing many "wormholes" [14, 15]. It has been proposed that travel by subatomic particles (I give you Aunt Dorothy's memory for example) may take place through these little tunnels. If the wormholes connect to other universes such as those postulated by Linde, then Aunt Dorothy could be saved from our collapsing universe. This being the case, then physicist Gerard t'Hooft of Utrecht University, who argues that it is impossible for any information under any circumstances to be lost [cited in 11], would be spared the embarrassment of being wrong. The information representing Aunt Dorothy would simply have tunneled to another universe instead of getting smoothed out at the point of singularity in ours.

Now, suppose Aunt Dorothy is nervous about wormhole travel and refuses to make the trip. If so, she might choose another way of allowing her memory and consciousness to escape a Big Crunch. She might select the method of "non-locality communication" (already mentioned in this chapter) which is the instant communication referred to by Einstein as "spooky action at a distance" [8, 9]. One may speculate that non-locality communication could have the potential to save Aunt Dorothy's memory and consciousness from getting squeezed down to nothing. Non-locality communication might instantly transfer them to another universe that is stable and far away.

We have been investigating possible methods in the above paragraphs for Aunt Dorothy to save herself in a collapsing universe. Someday it will become clear if all of these ideas are nonsense or if any of them might hold a grain of truth.

REGENERATING CONSCIOUSNESS

Have we saved Aunt Dorothy for immortality? Not yet. If Aunt Dorothy is to be saved, both her memory *and* consciousness must survive. Without the existence of both, we would not recognize her, nor would she recognize herself.

Why do I make a point of distinguishing between memory and consciousness as if they are not the same thing? Answer: because they are not.

We have said little about consciousness so far. Memory is one thing but consciousness is something quite different. Without what we call consciousness, there is no sense of self at all even if memory patterns continue to be present. For example, when we faint we lose consciousness. We lose the awareness of our senses and our memories. But as mentioned before, memory patterns are hard-wired components of the brain, fixed in space and time. They are not lost when we faint. We just lose our awareness of them. After regaining consciousness, we are once more aware of our memories because they have remained in our nerve networks in spite of fainting. It was only consciousness that was lost from our brain.

Now, let's take a closer look at consciousness. What causes it? How do we define it? How can it be saved for eternity?

Unlike past memory, which I have pictured as a relatively static pattern of nerves, consciousness is a dynamic, ongoing process [16]. Consciousness is the electrical activity in the brain that retrieves information from the memory. For example, when you think: "I had bacon for breakfast this morning," that is your consciousness at work retrieving information from the memory of an event that took place earlier in the day.

Consciousness can obtain information, not only from the memory, but also from the senses as, for example, the sense of taste. For instance, "I am enjoying the taste of this bacon right now" is your consciousness retrieving information from your taste buds.

We are talking here about consciousness because we want to know how Aunt Dorothy could be conscious in her new life if her brain is dead. Are the flesh and blood that make her conscious in life transportable to subatomic space? Obviously not. Flesh and blood are too big to fit into the subatomic world. They could not be contained in such a small region. Then how might Aunt Dorothy remain conscious in death without the structures that make her conscious in life? It is because consciousness consists of voltage changes, and these can be reproduced at another place. This exact pattern of voltages, even somewhere else, can theoretically be regenerated without the aid of the brain. For those readers who have the interest and patience, the manner in which this might be done is analyzed in chapter 5 of this book.

At this point, may I draw your attention to what two well-known investigators, both interested in consciousness, have to say about it?

One of these investigators is Nobel laureate Francis Crick (co-discoverer of DNA) who says that, rather than being supernatural, consciousness is simply the result of the movement of electricity in the brain. Crick says: "Consciousness is based solely on the interaction of neurons. Your joys, your sorrows, your memory and your ambitions, your sense of personal identity and free will, are in fact no more than the behavior of a vast assembly of nerve cells and their associated molecules" [17].

The other well-known Nobel laureate that I will mention is Roger Penrose whose ideas differ from Crick's. Penrose doubts that our rapid insights, leaps of intuition, and creativity could be induced by voltage changes in the brain. He suspects that quantum mechanics is at work [18]. According to Penrose, thoughts may exist in a number of superposed states. This means that different thoughts in the brain are existing at the same moment, overlapping one another as it were. For instance, a thought may exist that the sky is blue, and at the same time another may exist that the sky is green. When (in quantum mechanics jargon) the "wave function collapses," we are conscious of only one of these thoughts, the blue sky or the green sky. Not both. Put another way, either the green sky or the blue sky clicks into the awareness envelope (as consciousness is called) as a single thought. Penrose points to the little structures in cells called microtubules as possible sources of this quantum thought process.

Does either Penrose's or Crick's idea of consciousness fit into my Saved Consciousness Hypothesis? No, because the hypothesis is about consciousness in subatomic space after death. Neither Penrose's microtubules, nor Crick's neurons, are small enough to squeeze into the dimensions of subatomic space. Not even close. You can push and shove all you want, but you can't get neurons or microtubules in there. Although consciousness depends on brain structures in life, it must depend on something else in death.

Now, if Aunt Dorothy is to be conscious after death, and if she is to reside in the subatomic world, then there must be a way (according to this author) of getting her consciousness into subatomic space without involving microtubules or neurons. Is this possible? The Saved Consciousness Hypothesis says yes, it is possible. It suggests that there is a way that the process of consciousness can be transferred without violating any law of physics. Again, we will discover the details in chapter 5.

Meanwhile, there are other important parts of the hypothesis that I would like to put in place for you before focusing on the technical challenge of transferring consciousness from the brain networks to a subatomic domain.

We have, up to this point, looked at two ideas of a hypothesis predicting immortality. They are: *It is theoretically possible to transfer any kind of information from one place to another,* and *The subatomic world of quantum dimensions may be the region to which our memories and consciousness are transferred.*

But there is something missing here. Do you see what it is? I believe we need to add a third vital component to the Saved Consciousness Hypothesis if it is to make any sense. The third element has to do with preserving the *total* memory and consciousness of our whole life for recall after death. Total recall, not just bits and pieces.

Continuous Transfer

Our life is somewhat like a movie film. The things we see, hear, taste, smell, feel, and think are recorded every second, not actually on a film or tape, but rather in our memory. The recordings of all these details are not permanent [19, 20]. The fine points become weakened, then finally disappear. Only a few things remain in our memory for a long time. We lose the recall of most of the events that we have experienced during our lives. They cannot be retrieved even under hypnosis [21].

If you reflect upon this, you may disagree.

"I've got a pretty good memory," you say. "I remember most things."

Yes, you do for a while. But think carefully. Of all the words you have read in books, magazines, newspapers, letters, and elsewhere, do you recall each and every word? I doubt it.

Back in medical school, my anatomy professor told our class that we would be lucky if we remembered 20 percent of the material we studied from our textbook. He was right. Most of the students remembered much less than that (you should see the size of those textbooks!).

The information went in, but only a little of it was retained long term. Although the information that the brain receives through the senses is immediately registered in the memory, most of it stays for only seconds or milliseconds. For example, do you remember the shape of every flower, of every blade of grass you have ever seen in your life? Of course not. You would be a very unusual person if you did. Nevertheless, these images were once briefly registered in your brain.

The point I am making here is that by far the greatest part of our recall soon leaves our brains like a phone number that is used only once and then is no longer needed. In fact, at the moment of our death there is very little memory of the seconds of our lives left in the memory circuits. Our ongoing identity formed by our memory has holes in it. That necklace has lost most of its beads.

Now, the events of our past life could have significance for two possible scenarios after death (Appendix I). The first is how they might relate to a new life of new experiences. The second is what role they play in a recycled life.

Let's think, first, about having a brand new life after death. A life of new experience quite different from our past life. Forget, for the moment, about the recycling of the Saved Consciousness Hypothesis and think instead about having new experiences different to whatever has gone before. If this were to happen, it is possible to imagine that the memories of our old life would still contribute to our ongoing identity. Part of a continuum. If we could be conscious of every detail of our old life, every flower that we have seen, every word that we have read, it is my conjecture that our new identity would be considerably enriched by these memories.

Now, instead of thinking about a new life of different experiences, let's think about recycling our past life. Recycling means the regeneration of consciousness precisely as it occurred the first time around. We don't just select different moments to remember but, on the contrary, we actually live the old life over again.

We have, then, two scenarios. The first is a brand new post-mortem life with the retention of precise memories of the old. The second is simply recycling the old with no new life added. In the first scenario, if the new life is to be maximally enriched, then every single past experience must be recorded for reference. In the second scenario, if the old life is to be lived again to precision, then again every single past experience must be recorded for regeneration.

Both scenarios require a total, detailed recording of our past life.

This total recapture is made theoretically possible by the third element of the Saved Consciousness Hypothesis, which states:

> The memory patterns and flow of consciousness are being automatically recorded (at a subatomic location) continuously from birth to death, available for re-activation after death.

Transferred not once, but *continuously*. This means that each and every identity that is "us" at each moment of our life is preserved. Let's look at this idea more carefully.

We all know that people change from day to day because their new experiences affect the way they think and feel. For example, a person does not have the same sense of self in middle and old age as he or she had at birth or as a toddler. Every stage in life brings a new Self. Our sense of identity at eighty is not the same as it was at twenty. Which one of these Selves, toddler or old age, represents the true "us"? Which one would we like to take with us when we die? Which Aunt Dorothy, as she moves through her years from birth to death, is the one that is preserved for eternity?

The third element of the Saved Memory Hypothesis makes it unnecessary to choose. We take them all. It proposes that each of these Selves is saved. Each Self is synthesized from moment to moment by the living senses, memory, and consciousness, and each one of these moments, or Selves, is saved because the memories and entire voltage wave representing consciousness during our life has been recorded in subatomic space.

Now, what about the beginning and the end of life? Are the events that happen to us in our mother's womb recorded? And how about the events that happen to us during the dying process? Let's take these in sequence, beginning with consciousness in the womb.

Inside your mother's uterus, floating in warm amniotic fluid, there is presumably not much to be conscious of. The fetus, meaning three months to term [23], probably gains its sense of self very, very slowly. Consciousness must arise at the pace of a snail. First of all, the brain has to develop its billions of nerves and connections in order to make consciousness possible, and that takes time. These nerve networks in the brain process the electrical impulses brought into it from the senses, such as those of hearing, touch, pressure, and pain (it's depressing to think that one could feel pain at such an early age!). Like the brain, the senses also form gradually. Eventually, the senses are able to send electrical signals to the developing brain, and the brain is presumably able to process them to form early consciousness.

Until that time arrives, there are no senses and no brain to produce consciousness. Thoughts and feelings are logically absent. Without senses and brain, there is nothing to transmit information such as pressure and pain and nothing to receive and process it. Therefore, there are grounds to assume that consciousness is not present before the senses and brain are working together to produce thoughts and feelings. After that time, it is logical to believe that consciousness would, indeed, be present. For example, we commonly see babies born before the normal term, and these "preemies" have brains that are quite able to support consciousness.

What would the developing fetus be conscious of in the balmy fluid of the womb? There are sounds: the mother's heartbeat, the squishing and rumbling of her intestines, the dog barking in the outside world. And there are feelings: those of pressure on the fetus, perhaps the occasional cramp in the developing intestines, maybe a vague sensation of taste, the position of the limbs. This is not much, but it is something.

But wait. What's happening now to upset this relative peace? Suddenly the senses receive a deluge of new and extraordinary signals! The five senses are bombarded in every imaginable way as this small living creature is forced through the birth canal by the contracting uterus, maybe even dragged out with forceps. The soothing fluid is gone, the cord is cut, the baby's bum perhaps gets whacked, it takes its first breath and yells in protest. The shocked and insulted infant is now experiencing an entirely new level of consciousness.

So much for the development of consciousness at life's beginning. What about the other end of life, the time of death?

The end (death) can come quickly or slowly. Quick would be the guillotine, slow would be Alzheimer's (more about that in a minute). Now, some might ask: is a person subjectively aware of the death process itself? My answer would be yes, as long as he or she remains conscious. Consciousness relies on brain function, and death takes brain function away. It is only when you lose consciousness that you are no longer aware of the death process. Consciousness may be altered in the process by medications, chemical imbalances, hallucinations, and delusions. The apparitions that appear to some people close to death ("Near Death Experiences") are possibly brought about by changes to the consciousness induced by chemical abnormalities in the brain.

We see, then, that we may be conscious at the extreme ends of life, both in the womb and while dying. How does this square with the Saved Conscious Hypothesis and its postulate of the continuous transfer of consciousness to subatomic space?

There is no conflict. The Saved Consciousness Hypothesis fits both ends of life equally well. Simply put, the Hypothesis proposes that consciousness is recorded in subatomic space from the time of its first stirrings in the fetus's developing brain until the end of life when the last vestiges of the consciousness voltages permanently leave the brain.

Recall After Alzheimer's

The significance of the idea of continuous transfer and preservation, rather than transfer only at death, is better seen if we look at the memory loss that can be caused by brain disease.

For example, the reader may know of one or more people that have had Alzheimer's dementia, a devastating sickness that eventually kills its victim. It is a condition in which normal brain cells are destroyed and replaced by an accumulation of a useless material called beta amyloid [24].

The writer has lost two close friends from this catastrophic illness that wipes out the memory and cripples one's ability to function. At first you forget where the light switch is in the hallway, then you are unable to recognize your wife, your brother, your friends. You don't remember how to dress, eat, or go to the bathroom. You feel bewildered, confused, desperate. You are back to your infancy, totally dependent on help from others for every need.

Is this pitiful scrap of memory left in the brain of the dying Alzheimer's patient the only thing that will be salvaged for post-mortem existence? If so, then that person's original identity has been lost. But not to worry. The third element of the Saved Consciousness Hypothesis makes the loss of memory at the end stage (or any stage) of life a non-issue. All memories and consciousness of all stages of past life have been transferred. They were transferred continuously during life. That is the postulate of my Saved Consciousness Hypothesis. In other words, falling victim to Alzheimer's disease (a condition that would wipe out the living memory) would not in any way affect memory information that had already been transferred to subatomic space. The living person that loses his or her recall at any stage of life would, in effect, be given everything back at death.

I can almost hear someone say: "Why does this author persist in thinking that I want my memories back? I am interested in the future, not the past."

My answer is simple. If there is a new future, that does not mean we want to lose our past. We've gone through the difficult work of living our past life during which we have learned a lot and constructed our present identity. The identity has been built up of many parts. With total memory preservation, all these parts, or individual identities, would remain with us in our new life. This rich memory could serve as a familiar and welcome stepping-stone from which to face an otherwise unknown future.

And suppose, on the other hand, that there is no future and no fresh experience following death. After all, we have noted that there is no physical evidence either for such a future, or against it. In such a case, what do we have? My Hypothesis predicts, at very least, we have our past life to live again. This presumes that there exists in subatomic space a recording of every detail of our life, which upon regeneration would permit our life to be experienced again. In other words, even if my Hypothesis is unable to propose a *new* future, it at least can predict that we will not lose our past life. Continued consciousness would be assured.

Let's summarize.

In the brain, the memory is a place in which every event, every emotion, every thought, and feeling is registered, however briefly, in the same detail as it was originally sensed and felt. And yet, only the smallest fraction of all this information that once came to the brain is permanently held there. By far the greatest amount is degraded or lost. Thus, when we arrive at the point of death, our past life is only a poorly remembered, shadowy thing consisting of a few fragments of what we once knew. Just a tiny fraction remains of the incalculable number of events that were received by the brain in a steady stream throughout life.

However, the Saved Conscious Hypothesis with its proposal of ongoing transfer comes to the rescue. This writer, in his exalted position as creator of plausible or implausible scenarios, postulates that our memory and consciousness are being automatically relocated from the brain during every moment of life by incremental transfer or, better still, continuous transfer. That is what the third element of his Hypothesis states. That is why nothing is lost. All information as it registers in the brain is, at the same time, being transmitted to its alternative site in the subatomic quantum domain. Everything that we have ever seen, heard, thought, or felt. In this way, every detail of our hard-won past is available to us for regeneration. It is proposed that this automatic transfer is accomplished by a normal physical process that does not break any known natural law.

Now, let's briefly compare this supposed process of saving brain memory to the act of saving computer memory. To guard against the loss of data that we put into a computer, we may transfer it from time to time to an external storage medium such as a disk. In this way, as we put new information into the computer, it can be relocated as a duplicate to a safe place (disk) for permanent storage. Similarly, when we think about transferring memory and consciousness out of the fleshy brain, we may imagine God seated at His divine mainframe leaning on the save button so that every memory and consciousness pattern at every microsecond of each individual's life is preserved at a safe place. Kept safely in all its original detail at a new storage site.

If the recycling proposals in my Hypothesis are correct, then we are alive after death because, at a minimum, we can potentially relive our past life in faithful detail. We would smell, taste, see, hear, and feel as we did in our former life because everything we ever sensed, every thought in our brain, could be made to occur again. We would feel that we were using our muscles and exercising our free will as we did in life. During the regeneration, we would be re-experiencing life and know nothing of death. We might not even be aware that we were recycling memories and consciousness, and in fact be under the impression that we were living life for the first time. Exactly the same memory and consciousness circuits, although in a new place and built with new materials, would be as active as when we were sensing the experiences in real life for the first time. If you once walked with your friend on a certain street at a certain hour, you would be doing so once more. You wouldn't be merely watching, you would be actually doing it.

If you are still with me, you have now read about the three elements of the Saved Consciousness Hypothesis. For your reference, I would like to list them again:

First. There is a theoretical possibility during life of deploying and preserving memory and consciousness from the brain to some location independent of the brain.

Second. This independent location is in subatomic space.

Third. The memory patterns and flow of consciousness are being automatically recorded at this subatomic location continuously from birth to death, available for re-activation after death.

How true is all this? A hypothesis, by definition, is only a guess. When it comes to the Saved Consciousness Hypothesis, I have taken information that we know to be true and extrapolated from it into the realm of the totally unknown. I have taken facts, and tried to find out where they could lead us. For example:

1. We know it's possible to transmit a stored pattern (such as a recorded version of Ravel's Bolero) from point A to B. We have yet to test whether brain memory (a stored pattern) and consciousness (a dynamic pattern) are transmissible.
2. We know from experimental evidence that the subatomic quantum world is real. It remains to be tested whether or not it could house memory and consciousness patterns transferred from the brain.
3. We know that consciousness is created every time a brain is made. We don't know if consciousness together with memory could function in the small dimensions of the quantum world.

The *knowns* listed above are the facts we work from. The *unknowns* are waiting for future research. As science continues to reveal to us how our world works, a means for testing these unproven elements is likely to materialize.

SPECULATIONS

Now let's have ourselves a little fun by imagining what it might be like to be alive after death in the multiple dimensions of the quantum domain.

A New Body

Even if our Self lived among the quarks and leptons of a subatomic world, we would find that a "resurrected" fleshy body couldn't. For one thing, as we have previously noted, it wouldn't fit. For another, none of our body parts would work in the new environment because the physical laws are quite different there. Of what use would arms, legs, eyes, and ears be to a being existing inside, or between, atoms? If the post-mortem Self needs a body at all, it might be the size of a light photon, have no recognizable shape, and be both particle and wave. It is safe to say that the body we have in this life does not accompany us beyond the grave to a subatomic world. However, it could continue to exist in all its detail in our transferred memory. In that sense, according to my Hypothesis, our body would not be lost.

New Dimensions

It has been said that quantum space contains up to eleven dimensions. We are used to dealing with only four in our earthly lives: three in space and one in time. Although eleven dimensions are mathematical abstractions, so too at a fundamental level are the space-time dimensions in which we live. If we were to find a brand new life (as opposed to a recycled one) of fresh experience in the subatomic world, the radically different environment may take some getting used to. Perhaps there are all sorts of stunning wonders to find that will expand our identity. We will become someone new while remembering the old. I wonder if this is happening to Aunt Dorothy.

Resequencing

The Saved Consciousness Hypothesis, which is about recycling the past, presents another possibility. It is possible that there is a vast reservoir of new experience superposed on our consciousness wave that has not been precipitated out. According to quantum theory, Aunt Dorothy (and each one of us) potentially has an infinite number of different lives included in the waveform that represents us as an individual. This is inferred by the theory of quantum mechanics wave function. According to quantum theory, the wave function (which contains an infinite number of events) collapses at each instant of time to form a single event, and these single events add up to form the life we have lived.

It's fun to speculate that, upon a post-mortem replay of our life, any one of these superposed events might be selected (by an unseen hand) to replace the one that actually happened, and this would lead to a completely different life. There would be a new wave form of altered voltages. For example, when we turned right in real life, we might turn left on replay and that could lead to other outcomes (you might meet a blonde instead of a brunette, and marry him or her). If one considers that every point in life has the potential for a different decision and therefore a different outcome, there would be the opportunity for an almost unlimited number of unlived lives to be led. The objection that recycling simply involves mindless repetition would be refuted.

Other People

When and if we survive death to lead a new life (not just a recycled one), shall we be alone? It seems unlikely. Nature abhors uniqueness. If one person's memory and consciousness can be trans-located, presumably others can also. Would these new beings communicate with each other? They have no tongues, vocal cords, nor ears. We must wonder how they would exchange thoughts.

Conclusion

In the musings under this heading of "speculations," we have imagined some of the conditions one might (and might not) encounter in a post-mortem world. You need hardly be reminded that it is, of course, pure fantasy to make conjectures about new events for which we have no evidence. The Saved Consciousness Hypothesis, however, says little about new events after death, only about recycled ones. This Hypothesis is arrived at by extrapolation from what is known rather than being based exclusively upon imagination, intuition, and anecdote. To find truth, a hypothesis must be testable. A useful hypothesis will be built on a foundation of fact and indicate directions for future research. We will have to await further developments in science to discover whether or not the Saved Consciousness Hypothesis is testable.

The sequel to this presentation of the Saved Consciousness Hypothesis is coming up in chapter 5, and that is where we take a harder look at the potential for testing the predictions of the Saved Consciousness Hypothesis.

First, however, there are certain other things about death that you may wish to look at with me in the next two chapters.

REFERENCES

1. D. Dennett, *Consciousness Explained*, Little Brown & Co., Massachusetts, 1992.

2. A. R. Damasio and H. Damasio, Brain and Language, *Scientific American,* p. 91, September 1992.
3. G. D. Fischbach, Mind and Brain, *Scientific American,* pp. 48-57, September 1992.
4. N. Wiener, *The Human Use of Human Beings,* Avon Books, New York, 1950.
5. A. Zeilinger, Quantum Teleportation, *Scientific American,* pp. 50-59, April 2000.
6. F. Jorgensen, *Handbook of Magnetic Recording,* Tab Books, Pennsylvania, 1970.
7. D. Fawcett, *The Cell,* W. B. Saunders, New York, 1981.
8. D. Albert, *Quantum Mechanics and Experience,* Harvard University Press, Massachusetts, pp. 61-111, 1992.
9. J. Horgan, Quantum Philosophy, *Scientific American,* pp. 94-104, July 1992.
10. R. Omnes, *Understanding Quantum Mechanics,* Princeton University Press, New Jersey, 1999.
11. M. Mukerjee, Gathering String, *Scientific American,* p. 16, June 1994.
12. P. Yam, Writing on the Fringe, *Scientific American,* p. 40, October 1995.
13. A. Linde, The Self-Reproducing Inflationary Universe, *Scientific American,* pp. 48-55, November 1994.
14. K. S. Thorne, *Black Holes & Time Warps,* W. W. Norton & Co., New York, pp. 54-56, 1994.
15. D. Deutsch and M. Lockwood, The Quantum Physics of Time Travel, *Scientific American,* pp. 68-74, March 1994.
16. F. Crick and C. Koch, The Problems of Consciousness, *Scientific American,* p. 152, September 1992.
17. F. Crick, *The Astonishing Hypothesis,* Charles Scribner's Sons, New York, p. 3, 1994.
18. D. H. Freedman, Quantum Consciousness, *Discover Magazine,* pp. 89-98, June 1994.
19. E. R. Kandel and R. D. Hawkins, The Biological Basis of Learning and Individuality, *Scientific American,* pp. 78-86, September 1992.
20. A. R. Damasio and H. Damasio, Brain and Language, *Scientific American,* pp. 88-95, September 1992.
21. W. Weiten, *Psychology,* Brooks/Cole, California, p. 42, 1992.
22. M. R. Nash, The Truth and the Hype of Hypnosis, *Scientific American,* pp. 53-55, July 2000.
23. N. B. Taylor (ed.), *Stedman's Medical Dictionary* (17th Edition), Williams & Wilkins, Baltimore, p. 430, 1949.
24. P. H. St George-Hyslop, Piecing Together Alzheimer's, *Scientific American,* pp. 76-83, December 2000.
25. D. J. Selkoe, Aging Brain, Aging Mind, *Scientific American,* pp. 134-142, September 1992.

CHAPTER 3

Meet the Grim Reaper

In this chapter, we are going to look at death. As we know, an individual's life is a sequence of events beginning with the union of egg and sperm and ending in an encounter with the Grim Reaper. Death arrives when the cells of the body stop functioning, no matter what the reason may be. In higher animals, this of course means that the cells can no longer support consciousness and as a result the animal loses its sense of self in the ordinary world. The Grim Reaper draws the line separating one's self in life and what we suppose may be an afterlife.

The focus of this book is the afterlife and the Saved Consciousness Hypothesis. However, the transition point we call death merits, I believe, some special attention. We will consider it separately. In this chapter, I will attempt to show that this transition point is not necessarily a one-way street, not a final point of no return. In certain cases a living entity can, like Lazarus, die and come back from the dead.

As a first order of business, I would like to invite you to join me in an imaginary bit of juggling where we take the body apart and put it together again. Next, we will follow an actual procedure in which the life is taken away from a single cell and then given back so that the cell is fully alive once more. We will be playing with life and death to try and find out more about the mystery of death. If some of the mystery is removed, perhaps there will be less reason to fear death. That is what this chapter is about.

THE DEATH AND REBIRTH OF THE BODY (A THOUGHT EXPERIMENT)

Let's do something different. Why don't we put aside the way we normally look at death (at least for a moment) and look at it with its clothes off. Let's look at death as if it was not a bogeyman, a horror, but simply a mechanical process. So we will now attempt to strip the clothes off the Grim Reaper and see what's underneath.

What, actually, is death? Let's do a little thought experiment that should help us look at death in a different light than we are accustomed to viewing it. We will use an original perspective. Let's spread the body out in dishes.

When you look at the body through a microscope, you see that it is made up of tiny compartments called cells [1]. Each cell is like a miniature room packed full of complicated machinery. Most of the rooms are firmly attached to each other but without doors or windows. When we look at these cells, we are looking at the simplest forms of true life [2]. Viruses are simpler but may not qualify as life.

Cells, in a certain sense, are individuals. Like the whole body, they are born, they live, and they die. Now here is the point that I want to make about these basic units of life (I know you're waiting for it). It is that *each cell of the body, your body, can live separately, independently, from the other cells,* and also, of course, die a separate death. Each little room, as it were, can be separated from its neighbor, placed in a dish and allowed to live its own, separate life that has nothing to do with the body where it once lived. It's now on its own. In other words, each of the trillions of cells that make up the body can, theoretically, be placed in its own little dish and, given the proper nutrients, flourish.

The thought experiment I have proposed, then, is to spread the body out in dishes. Disassemble all the little cells that are normally attached to one another and permit them to live in complete isolation from each other, one per dish. Now if we do this, it is clear that the body is long gone. It is not a body anymore. By analogy, if you remove the bricks from a brick building, it is no longer a building. The various cells of the body are now living in separate dishes and no longer cooperate to form a body.

Can a person disappear just like that? Why not? The body didn't vanish into thin air; it was just taken apart, but the *parts are still alive.* The not-so-efficient Grim Reaper killed the person, but not the parts. What's going on here?

Let's probe further. If the body has died, at what point did it die? Did it die by degrees? How many cells must be removed before the doctor will sign the death certificate? One, three, a billion cells? The answer is this. When enough cells have been removed to *permanently* stop the brain functioning, then the person will be pronounced dead. Brain dead, person dead. Since we removed all the cells and put them into their own separate dishes, then obviously the brain, which no longer exists as a brain, is dead. So we conclude that the person is dead. This seems fair. But is that person permanently dead, or is there such a thing as temporary death? Does the Grim Reaper ever allow death to turn back into life?

Let's look at this question carefully. We've gone this far, so we've nothing to lose in this slightly weird thought experiment by going a step farther. We'll attempt to put the body together again. Let's reassemble the parts and see what happens. Isn't imagination great?

Suppose we go around to all the little dishes, take out the individual cells, and allow them to get together and attach themselves to one another, each in its former place. It is theoretically possible for them to rebuild the body. Each cell attaches to its original neighbor and lo! Magic! Not only are the cells alive and well but so is the body. The so-called Grim Reaper is not so grim after all. We have a living person, the same one we started with. It walks, it talks, it thinks, it remembers, it is conscious and knows who it is.

What has been done? First the Reaper apparently killed the person by taking the body apart, but then gave the person back life and consciousness by reassembling the parts. The parts never died, but the body did, then it was restored to life. This thought experiment indicates that death can be temporary. The body ceases to exist, but only temporarily. What does this tell us? Simply that death is not as clear-cut as we might have thought.

True, this has all been imaginary. And yet, we can take an example from real life that is not as extreme, but I think it will serve to get the point across that a body can be taken apart and put together again. There is a small marine creature called the Volvox [3, p. 643]. You can read about it in almost any Zoology textbook. It is made up of individual cells that can leave and reattach themselves to the main body at will. In other words, parts of the main body can disassemble, swim away, and then put themselves together once more. The individual cells appear to be free to come and go as they please and live either independently or as part of the main body. This differs from our thought experiment because, in the Volvox, only some of the cells leave the main body. In the thought experiment, however, we went to the extreme point of removing all of the cells before re-assembling them. In the case of the Volvox, I don't think it is known how many cells must leave before the body can no longer function as such.

Now, what about the life and death of the cells themselves? The single cells that form our body? When a cell dies, is it a permanent death? That depends on how it dies, as we shall see.

THE DEATH AND RESURRECTION OF THE CELL (AN ACTUAL EXPERIMENT)

Let's focus our attention on a single living cell, say one that we remove from the skin, liver, or any other part of the body. This time we are going to leave the remainder of the cells in the body alone and concentrate on just this one cell. The body does not even notice the absence of a single living cell, and obviously won't be hurt by its loss. After all, we shed billions of them every day [1].

Now ask ourselves a question. If we kill this cell, say by freezing it solid, is the death we have caused a permanent death or can the cell be made to live again? Is it possible in the real world to kill, then resurrect the dead thing as we did in our thought experiment with the whole body?

The answer is yes [4]. It can be done very easily. This is how.

Normally, a cell is kept alive by its own internal machinery. This internal machinery takes in food, excretes wastes, and produces energy (Appendix V). If the machinery within the cell grinds to a stop for any reason, then the cell quickly dies. No ifs, no buts. The cogs and wheels grind to a halt inside the cell, and this basic unit of life is dead. Now, this is exactly what happens if we freeze the cell. Everything inside stops moving. No food assimilation, no waste excretion, no energy production. No working machinery, no chemistry, no life. We look at the cell, and pronounce it dead.

But is it dead? What we usually mean when we say dead is dead forever. But a cell that died from freezing is not necessarily dead forever. Its life can be restored. We are now going to do something, and you probably know what, that will turn death back to life.

We are not dealing here with a thought experiment. Bringing death back to life is done routinely in the lab. First you freeze the cell so that all its machinery comes to a standstill. Then by magic, or so it seems, you bring this totally dead cell back to life again. What magic wand do you wave? You simply apply heat. You thaw the cell out, unfreeze it, and behold! It lives again, going about its normal business as though it had not just crossed the barrier between life and death. The cell's machinery starts up spontaneously without any supernatural intervention. Heat alone does it. Life, death, then life, in that order. No black magic, merely the physics of nature. The Reaper has been foiled.

Just in case you have lost track, we are talking here about the fact that death is not necessarily final. We have been watching how the Grim Reaper works. We have imagined death of the whole body by placing its individual cells one by one in separate dishes, and resurrecting the body by reuniting the cells. The death of the body was not permanent. Then, doing a real experiment, we actually killed a single cell by freezing it, and brought the cell back to life with heat. Again, death was only a transitory state. The reader may think, "But the cell was not really dead, was it? It was only frozen." Which makes us ask, what is death?

When all movement stops within the cell, that cell is dead. The cell we froze could remain frozen for a minute, a year, or a million years. During the time it is frozen, there is no evidence that its molecules are moving or functioning in any way. All function has stopped. The cell is merely an inanimate object without any sign of what we call life. It is inert like a stone. The difference is, the dead cell can come back to life again if we choose to unfreeze it because it has a structure that will support life. The stone doesn't.

Is it better to say that the frozen cell is in a state of "suspended life," instead of calling it dead? Is there a difference between suspended life and death? We are apparently just playing games with words, labeling an apparent distinction that does not really exist. The frozen cell maintains a structure that once supported life. Warm it up and life returns. Try warming up a frozen stone, and see what happens. You will obviously not make it live because a stone does not have the required architecture to support life and never did. In conclusion it is safe to say that, if we kill a single cell by freezing it, the death need not be permanent. Although we brought everything to a "dead" stop, we were able to start it again. In this case, the Grim Reaper can only visit, but not stay.

BODY FREEZING

Before leaving the subject of freezing, suppose we briefly look at a question that we hear talked about and that may intrigue some readers. The question is this: can we freeze a whole human body, and bring it back to life sometime later? Restore life perhaps in a year, two years, a thousand years in the future? Theoretically yes, but practically, not yet.

Why not? If it can be done with a single cell, why not your whole body? Why can't your dead body be frozen to preserve it, then heated up again when someone has discovered a cure for the disease that killed you?

Well, it can't be done simply because we don't have the technology to do it. Certainly not at the present time. Let me explain.

The main reason that the whole body cannot be frozen and brought back to life is simply that ice crystals form between the cells when the tissue is frozen, and this ice rips the delicate tissues apart [4]. This devastation happens everywhere in the frozen body, not just in a few places. It happens in the brain, the muscles, the different organs. The tissues are destroyed at a microscopic level because cells themselves rupture wherever ice crystals are formed, the interior cell contents spill out, with the result that the damage is far too great for any chance of repair. The machinery that supports life is not just stopped—it is destroyed by the formation of ice crystals between cells and the rupture of the cells. Death of the body by freezing is a final death without any possibility of reversal, at least by today's technology. If you want to find immortality, I would suggest that a liquid nitrogen freeze is probably not the way to go.

This is unfortunate, not only for those who would like to reach immortality by this means, but also because surgeons cannot draw upon storage banks of frozen body parts to transplant into other people. Doctors would like to have frozen organs such as livers, kidneys, hearts, and so on stored long term in large organ banks for future transplantation. They would like to have these organs ready at hand, so there would be no waiting when a patient urgently needed a transplant. Unfortunately for the surgeon and the patient, no one knows how to store a whole organ by freezing it without destroying the organ due to the formation of ice crystals between its cells. Efforts to successfully freeze whole organs have been made by perfusing the organ with different types of antifreeze solutions called cryoprotectants, and to inject other types of solution to try and minimize the size of the ice crystals that form. So far, no cigar as they say, but the efforts continue. Researchers are still trying to find ways to freeze body organs without killing the cells that make them up.

At this point, you may be wondering why it is that single cells can be frozen successfully but not whole organs or the whole body. It is because single cells are not surrounded by other neighboring cells, so ice crystals can't form between cells. It is the water *between* cells that causes the trouble. Ice forms in the water between cells and can't go anywhere. Because ice expands when it forms, the cells suffer. You can get away with freezing small groups of cells, even thin sheets of cells that are used as skin grafts, but not whole organs, nor a whole body [4, 5].

Until researchers find a way to get around the problem of ice crystals, surgeons and patients alike will have to rely on the present method of storing organs, which is to refrigerate, not freeze, them. Refrigeration helps to prolong their life for a while, but is not the long-term solution that freezing would be if it were possible.

Now let's talk about killing an individual cell, not by freezing it, but by taking it apart. Our attention here is not on a whole body, not on a whole organ, but on a single cell. This will be another thought experiment (Einstein did them all the time!). Let's take the cell apart, break it down into its parts, its individual cogs and wheels, and separate them so the pieces of machinery can no longer work together to support the life of the whole cell. This can theoretically be done, for we have micropipettes that can suck out vital parts of the cell.

Let's say, then, that we kill the cell by removing its insides and separating all the different parts. That's easy enough. Now, a natural question pops up: would it be possible to put these cogs and wheels back together so that the cell can live again? Can the little cell, as we did with the whole body in a former thought experiment, be broken down into its individual parts so that the cell is dead, and then can the cell be made to live again by reassembling the parts? Can the various organelles such as the nucleus, mitochondria, endoplasmic reticulum, and Golgi Apparatus be removed from the cell, separated from each other, then re-injected back into the cell to re-generate life. Life, then death, then life again?

We cannot give a clear answer to this question. We have to fudge. Once again, as with the thought experiment where we put all the cells of the human body into individual dishes, death deals with numbers. How many cells do you have to remove from the body, whether human or Volvox, before it is pronounced dead? Likewise, how many cell organelles must be extracted from the single cell before the cell is pronounced dead? One, two, ten? The distinction between life and death is not an easy one to draw and may simply be a matter of degree. As always, one has to ask: death of what?

This chapter so far has been about getting to know the Grim Reaper. In order to know him better, the reader was given a thought experiment to do. It became evident from this thought experiment, and also from the study of a real life example (Volvox), that death of the body can occur without causing the death of the parts (cells), because they can exist separately, and that death of some parts (cells) can occur without causing the death of the whole body because it has many more cells than it needs for survival. We also noted that death could come when a single cell is frozen, and it can leave when the cell is thawed out. Thus, we see that death can be reversible. It is a strange thought, but the evidence supports it.

FEAR OF DEATH

Since this chapter is about death, I would like to talk a little about the fear of death that most of us have.

When we faint, or are given an anesthetic, or fall into a deep coma, we are not aware of ourselves during that time. Anticipating such a subjective lapse of existence does not devastate us because we believe that it is only a passing affair, that we will be conscious again, that everything will be as it was before.

But what about the loss of consciousness caused by permanent death? Now that is something else. From all the evidence we see about us during the normal course of our lives, death is the end, death is permanent, the fat lady sings, we are no more. And that means forever. This can be a scary thought to human beings who, perhaps uniquely in the animal kingdom, know they will die someday.

Why do we fear this? Are we justified in fearing death?

The late well-known and respected psychologist Carl Jung said that he never met a person over forty that did not fear death. If at some future time it is shown as a *fact,* not merely speculation, that consciousness and memory do survive death, that they do indeed exist beyond the death of the body, then humans may lose some of this apprehension. That is to say, if the Saved Consciousness Hypothesis that you read about in chapters 2 and 5, or if something similar is scientifically shown to be well founded, then there will be no reason for people to feel that death is the cutting off point of their existence.

Meanwhile, most people allay their natural fear of death by faith in their god. This has been the biggest source of comfort for humans throughout history. Most religions offer the promise of a soul that can be saved from oblivion, of an identity that is eternal [6]. So fear of death can be tempered by religion that offers the promise of everlasting existence. The Saved Consciousness Hypothesis likewise postulates eternal existence, but looks for verification in scientific terms to make the idea demonstrable.

However, science is a long way from testing the Saved Memory Hypothesis or anything like it. Science can offer no confirmation for life after death. Not yet. And as for religion, a belief in life after death is based on faith, scriptural anecdotes, and intuition. In other words, we have no facts to date, either from religion or other sources, that indicate beyond question whether or not our consciousness or memory exists after the brain expires. Most of us, for the present, will go on fearing death as we have always done, and this is why.

As I have noted, death looks to us like the annihilation of our identity. We guess that the world will continue to spin after our death, just as we speculate that the Sun will continue to shine, but so what? We won't be here, we won't be anywhere, as far as we know. We reason that our consciousness will expire when our brain is dead, so we won't know anything about the world, the Sun, or other things. Nature has made us fear this gaping void, this end to our consciousness, and of course it's a good thing that it has.

Our bodies and minds have been made in such a way that we instinctively fear death. It is an inborn fear in all thinking animals. It is combined with a fear of injury and pain. It is in our genes. The genes in our chromosomes instruct us to avoid death above all other things. That is their program. They direct us to avoid any sort of injury, and death is the ultimate injury.

If fear of death were not programmed in our genes, we would all be dead. We wouldn't produce any children to propagate our species because we wouldn't live long enough to reach puberty. I am stressing this obvious point to emphasize that psychological fear of death is not only normal, but also a necessary genetic trait. Without the fear of death, or injury, or pain, we as individuals would not be alive because the human race would never have multiplied and come to inhabit the Earth. As we know, the central idea in evolution is survival of the fittest, and the fittest have a fear of death. So don't feel too bad if you want to refuse that invitation for a morning of skydiving or bungee jumping. By saying no thanks, you will improve your chances of living long enough to create a new generation.

So, I think I have made my point. We have a fear of death, and it's what keeps us alive. How do we make peace with it?

Most of us are able to live with the fear of death quite well, and we don't usually let it get us down or seriously interfere with our lives. We are normally too busy for that. We make a pact with death. Let us live for a bit, we say. Let us do our thing while we can, meet our challenges, have some fun, and we won't be too concerned about death. We will deal with it when we have to. Most of us are just too busy keeping alive to think about death very much.

Now, despite our ability to make peace with death, wouldn't some of us like to delay the arrival of death for a bit, or perhaps even foil the Grim Reaper entirely? Can we do something to make ourselves immortal or, at very least, postpone our death? Would we want to do this? Do we want to postpone death? If we had the choice, would we want to live much longer than we do, or even eliminate death altogether?

Let's look at the idea of postponing death. As a matter of fact, it's something we all struggle to do every day but, unfortunately, have only developed modest skills at it. There is much room for improvement if we want to seriously hold the Grim Reaper at bay for longer than our expected lifetime. If you are curious and will accompany me to the next chapter, we will together investigate this idea of postponing death.

REFERENCES

1. A. W. Ham, *Histology,* J. B. Lippincott, Montreal, 1965.
2. D. Fawcett, *The Cell,* W. B. Saunders, New York, 1981.
3. R. W. Hegner, *College Zoology* (5th Edition), Macmillan, New York, 1947.
4. K. B. Storey and J. M. Storey, Frozen and Alive, *Scientific American,* pp. 92-97, December 1990.
5. D. E. Pegg and A. M. Karow, Jr., *The Biophysics of Organ Cryopreservation,* Plenum Press, New York, 1988.
6. H. Smith, *The Religions of Man,* HarperPerrenial (A Division of Harper Collins), New York, 1986.

CHAPTER 4

Postponing Death

It would be preposterous to think that we could postpone death forever. Or would it? Who knows? For practical purposes, in your life and mine, we will settle for a few more years.

In this chapter, we are going to talk about ways to postpone death. Some of these methods are quite familiar and we make good use of them on a daily basis. Other ways are being investigated at the present time with practical results still to come. Still other possibilities hold only a vague promise for the future.

EXTENDING THE LIFE SPAN

Most people on the planet in good physical and mental health would like to postpone death. This is quite evident. We don't intentionally do such things as walk off cliffs or jump out of airplanes (without chutes) because of the obvious fatal result. We are programmed to avoid that. We want to hold onto our good health. If we get sick with appendicitis or pneumonia, we see a doctor because we don't like being sick and we are not enchanted with the prospect of dying. Every additional day we live we have cheated death a little bit longer.

Not all people strive for a longer life. We know that unusual circumstances may overpower one's instinct for survival. For example, the fanatical desire to advance a personal cause may drive one to commit suicide, clearly evident in the recent suicidal hijacker destruction of the Twin Towers of the New York Trade Center. On the other hand, pain or sickness may compel the sufferer to seek relief in death. This tragic situation was given a high profile by pathologist Jack Kevorkian ("Dr. Death") in recent times. Also, depression, societal pressure, grief, or the willingness to end one's own life to save another may also provide the motivation to seek death. However, it is evident that these are exceptions to an otherwise universal rule: Generally speaking, we embrace life and want more of it.

You and I know how to postpone death for a while. We improve the odds of a long life by avoiding accidents and injuries. But here is the big question: can we postpone death by a major chunk? By that, I mean for hundreds, or say thousands, of years? Can we fiddle with the human body in order to engineer such a long life span?

This is important to know because having death waiting in the wings is stressful, and we have enough stress and worry in our lives without a constant wait for the Grim Reaper's unwanted visit. If death could be postponed—put off to some indefinite point far in the future; if we thought, for example, that we could live, say, for a thousand years barring normal accidents, then we would eliminate the death stress and gratefully step out from under the sword of Damocles.

Postponing death would not completely eliminate fear of death, but that's okay because, as has been said, the fear is programmed into our genes and is there to protect us. We need the fear, but not the worry. If, by taking intelligent precautions, we could postpone the inevitability of death to the distant future, an immediate burden would be lifted from our backs. The grim executioner would no longer be skulking about in the wings in ghoulish anticipation, sharpening his blade. Banning this perceived monster to the remote shadows would change our outlook on life. Most of us would heave a sigh of relief because that inevitable day of reckoning would be so far away that it would have little consequence for our daily lives. There may be those who say: "Ah, but the constant threat of death makes us appreciate life more and keeps us moral!" Well, we will get to that part later in the book.

Now, let's look at several ways that death could be postponed significantly, for a much longer time than we are used to thinking about. I am talking here about delaying death for hundreds or thousands of years. The time doesn't matter. If we find the method, it could be good for any length of time. If you think that it won't happen in your lifetime, you are probably right. Nevertheless, you never know. Look, you have seen amazing new developments recently in science. You have probably noticed that the pace of such developments is accelerating. The breakthroughs in science and technology are snowballing. These rapid advances are all part of the ongoing science that should make us live longer, perhaps indefinitely. I am confident that it will happen, but there is no telling when.

AGING

One good way to make such a breakthrough in the search for a long life is to do something about aging. This is a good place to start. We see our friends and relations getting long in the tooth and we know we will soon be going to their funeral, or they will be coming to ours. We're obviously all in the same boat and will expire from old age if we're lucky enough to live that long. Unless scientists can halt the degeneration of the body that goes on with the passage of time, then death from old age is a foregone conclusion.

Why does the body normally grow and flourish in good health until it has lived for twenty years or so, then begin to slide downhill until it becomes frail, sickly, and creaky? [1, pp. 125-223]. Is this gradual damage to the aging body really necessary? Could it be overcome?

Serious attention to these questions on the part of reputable biologists only came toward the middle of the last century [2, 3]. At that time, various laboratories began to spring up in order to work exclusively on the problems of aging. One such lab, for instance, was the Department of Gerontology in Baltimore, a division of the National Institutes of Health, where I personally worked as a medical graduate.

Even though the pace of research on biological aging has accelerated worldwide in the last half century, no practical breakthrough has surfaced to date. A lot of valuable information has accumulated, but the Fountain of Youth remains elusive. The animal kingdom still suffers from the misery of old bodies.

Now here is an important point. When the subject of extending the human life span comes up, there is always someone who makes the following objection: "Who wants to be old, diseased, weak, and crippled? I'd rather die first," they say. Of course you would. But who said anything about being diseased, weak, and crippled? We're talking here about finding a way to hold on to the young, healthy body of our youth. That's what it's all about. We seek a way to stay young, not in age, but in body! Beautiful women, handsome men, physically strong and mentally alert. Prolonging life for hundreds of years would be of little interest if it did not go with good health, vigor, and the strength of youth. The crippled body and demented mind is not what anyone wants to end their life with. The joy we get out of life comes in part from having a body and mind in top condition. That way we can meet our challenges and have some fun while we're at it.

Now, would it be possible to have it this way, to keep the body and brain of our younger days intact despite the passage of time? If so, then one couldn't care less about age. We would be old in years, yes, but wiser, and we would be young in body and mind. We would look forward to the future as the years passed, instead of dreading the infirmities of the so-called golden age which (ask any senior citizen) is not really so golden. With all our faculties in first-rate shape, life would remain a pleasurable challenge and I believe most of us would continue to embrace it.

"Ah," the critic objects. "I would be bored living so long. I'm starting to get bored now."

I don't think one can take this objection too seriously. Everyone is occasionally bored, but life as a rule is too exciting to grow tired of it. Remember, I am assuming the state of a youthful body and a healthy mind. There is just too much to do and discover in our Universe to allow us to grow weary of an extended life.

Now, down to the nuts and bolts. What causes aging? How can it be stopped, even reversed?

There are some every day, simple observations that we can make about aging that continue to baffle everyone, from layman to scientist. Let me give you what I think is a good example. We all take it for granted that there are wide differences in the life spans of various animals [3, pp. 55-157]. This is pretty obvious. The fruit fly, for instance, lives only about forty days. The rat does better than that, living for about three years. The dog (depending on the breed) does still better, lasting around a dozen years, while the human animal is expected to have a life span of at least seventy-five to eighty years.

There are other examples, of course, of even wider ranges of life span. Why is this so? Why these differences? As yet, nobody knows. The person or team that finds the answer will be able to postpone death. They and their methods, needless to say, will be very popular. In addition to prolonging the life span, they will have removed a major cause of disease, which is aging. They will be the toast of the town!

The answer to aging, many believe, will come because science rolls forward. As previously mentioned, research labs on aging and other aspects of biology, both public and private, are sprouting forth like tulips in the spring [1, pp. 372-391]. This frenzy has had a tremendous impact on the production of new drugs, new techniques, new ideas. Each advance relates to preceding ones, and we have a rolling snowball of exciting information that can be used to improve our lives. Our understanding gets bigger at an increasing rate. Our knowledge and the ability to put that knowledge to use advances exponentially.

I presently think, as I believe many workers do, that the answer to aging lies somewhere in the DNA molecules that reside in the cells of every animal. DNA contains the instructions of life, and in the DNA molecule there is the potential to control those elements that make our tissues age. We assume that some units in this molecule, or its protein products, decide the extent of an animal's lifespan. The reason that you and I are destined to live, on average, thirty times longer than a rat, seven hundred and fifty times longer than a fruit fly, may be found in our DNA.

The general structure of the DNA molecule was figured out by Watson and Crick in 1953 [4] and advances since then have given us a beautifully detailed picture of this molecule which, by replication, passes on characteristics from parent to child. Recent work by the independent teams of Collins and Venter has dotted the I's and crossed the T's. We now have a master blueprint of how the body, how each cell, works. The book of life is finally open at a very basic level. The letters and words are all exposed. What we have to do is learn how to read and understand them [5].

This chapter, in case I have caused you to lose focus, is about how to delay death. By slowing, or eliminating the aging process, we are delaying death and also disease. It would be nice to continue life with a young, vibrant body and mind beyond the presently accepted life span. There are ways to do this, some of them more practical than others, which I will now explain.

STOP-GAP MEASURES

When we are young, we have about a 90 percent reserve in most of our organ systems. That means that, in youth, we have a large surplus of tissue beyond our normal needs to support life. The body could scrape by on, say, 10 percent or so of the kidney tissue, lung tissue, liver tissue and what not that it possesses in youth. Nature is generous when we begin life. She gives us a big reserve for contingencies. She knows we will require this reserve to fight disease, injury, and aging. As the years roll by, this generous reserve is gnawed away by processes that we don't fully understand [1, pp. 125-223]. When we are very old, we are left with almost no reserve at all just when we need it most. In our advanced years, all organ systems may be working at full output merely to keep us alive. Any accident or disease that comes along can zap us. A new accident or disease will hit one or two of our over-taxed organ systems and put an impossible strain on other systems which themselves are struggling to keep up. What does this mean? Curtains! Along comes a slight health problem, and we collapse like a house of cards blown over by a sudden puff of wind.

The current way of managing this problem of reduced reserve in aging people is strictly stop-gap. Good medical intervention is usually able to come to the rescue, but the attempt seems somewhat pathetic. Doctors dole out a few more years of life to aging people by transplanting somebody else's liver, kidney, or heart into them. Or giving the patient kidney dialysis. Or feeding life-sustaining mush by stomach tube. They replace knees or hips with artificial devices, provide hearing aids, plastic heart valves, and so forth. This is the only available way at present, it seems, to manage the afflictions of old age.

What is the outlook for the future? It is better. New and improved methods of management will come along but they will still be stop-gap. One such management technique presently being worked out is the transplantation of stem cells [6]. Stem cells are cells in the body that are similar to the early cells that form the embryo in our mother's womb. These cells can miraculously change into any kind of tissue in the body such as heart, brain, or bone tissue. This of course is how we started out in life: a stem cell that divided into two, four, and then trillions. The stem cell that we began with differentiated into all the other different kinds of cells in our body. This ability of the stem cell to turn into any other kind of cell is a future hope, providing that ethical considerations can be successfully resolved. Stem cells can potentially be used to repair damage in any organ. Inject some stem cells into the damaged tissue, and they can theoretically fabricate healthy tissue to repair the damaged tissue. This, of course, is an obvious way to postpone death. For example, it is expected that stem cells might repair the brain damage in the Alzheimer's patient, or create new lung tissue, heart tissue, or bone tissue. Any tissue at all in the body. Be patient, however. This is a promise only, not a done deal.

Now, I wish to make what I think is an even more important point. How much better would it be if one were able to halt the aging process altogether? Stop aging. Not let the body crumble to the stage where it needs all these crutches to permit it to hobble to the next disease. Simply avoid the diseases of old age by staying young. In other words, maintain that 90 percent reserve of healthy tissue that prevents us from imploding like a salted snail at the slightest infection or other insult. Eliminate the need for stem cell replacement or any other stop-gap measure to combat the diseases of age. Just find a way to stop the aging process altogether. That, it seems to me, would be the best way to significantly postpone death and dangle before us the prospect of a happy future. Can it be done? Is it pie in the sky, or perhaps foolish fancy?

I for one believe it can be done. I think it is far from foolish fancy. The differences we see in the life spans of various animal species, including the human animal, tell us that there is something that regulates the life span [1, pp. 356-360]. The life span tends to be different for each species, from microbe to man. It is our job to find what regulates it.

So far, there are no successful theories explaining the action of the regulators. We simply don't know why animals age. We tinker at the fringes. We have hypotheses concerning such things as telomeres, free radicals, replication errors, diet restriction, radiation damage, toxins, wear and tear, disease damage, and so on, and all of these may play a role. But no successful theory has been proposed, and no cure is as yet in the pipeline. I think the cure and theory will come. Scientists working with DNA will find out what proteins made by DNA are involved in the aging process. They will design new proteins that will modify this process. I fully expect ways will be found to slow, stop, and even reverse, aging in the human body. You may live to enjoy it.

We have talked about aging as the big terminator of human lives. We would like to delay aging so we could be healthier and live longer. But age is not the only specter that threatens us. There are other nasty things out there that can cut our lives short such as accidents and wars. We have more control over them than we do over aging. Another menace is disease, and fortunately we seem to be gaining on this killer. Our life span has increased dramatically over the past century by successfully handling many infections, treating some cancers, slowing diabetes, and managing other diseases. As you know, we are still moving ahead on this front. There are scientists and inventors now dreaming about microscopic robots they call *nanobots* [7-9] that they would like to put in the blood stream to travel around the body like little submarines repairing tissues, fighting disease, and doing other useful things that they would be programmed to do. Nano means very small, something so small it can barely be seen with an electron microscope. Bot is short for robot. This all may sound supremely fanciful but perhaps it isn't when you consider where we are today in the miniaturization of microchip technology. The inventors predict that these nanobots will be placed in the blood stream by the billions where they will patrol the body for injury and disease. The blood will carry the nanobots to every corner of every organ. The nanobot will be programmed to identify and correct all problems that it encounters. Any abnormality in any tissue or cell will be found and repaired.

This, of course, is only a dream, and only one of many dreams to postpone death. It is encouraging to know that there are some very imaginative and clever people at the cutting edge of biotechnology today who can raise big bucks to back up their crazy-sounding ideas, some of which may not turn out to be so crazy after all. These guys often see possibilities in the future where others don't, and they frequently succeed in recruiting teams of other clever people to help them test their schemes. These and other imaginative investigators are, in effect, working to delay death.

We are talking in this section of the chapter specifically about postponing the arrival of the Grim Reaper. We know he's coming, but we are trying to hold him off. We have talked about keeping death at bay by tackling the aging problem and the disease problem. Are there other ways of extending life? Yes, and we have seen one of them when we talked about freezing cells. A frozen cell is a cell whose structure can be preserved for any length of time, as far as we know.

FREEZING

Today we are able to freeze single living cells or small groups of cells and thaw them out so that they live again. We saw in the last chapter that, when they are frozen, their life is suspended which means that they are dead but can be brought back to life. While frozen, the cell is simply an inanimate object like a piece of rock where nothing moves. Heat it up, and it is once again a living thing. Its death has been delayed [10].

Is there any length of time beyond which you cannot revive a cell that has been preserved by freezing? Probably not. Theoretically you could leave the cell frozen for a billion years during which time it would be dead, but not irreversibly so. After a billion years (is anyone keeping time?) you could apply heat and bring the cell back to life. In a sense, you have extended the cell's life span by a billion years.

This cannot be done with the human body, as we have seen. Current technology will not permit us to extend the human life span by freezing, even if we wanted to. We have noted that the ice crystals that form in the tissues destroy our cells beyond repair. Humpty Dumpty can't be put together again.

This does not mean that, at some future time, this extreme procedure could not be carried out successfully. Present technology does not permit it, but future methods might. We are getting better and better at lowering the temperature of flesh without the formation of damaging ice crystals. We are being pushed in this quest for lower temperatures because we want to preserve organs for transplant. If we can lower the temperature of, say, a kidney so it is low enough to stop metabolism, then the kidney can be stored for a long time and be transplanted later.

For this purpose, we have developed substances that work on the same principle as the antifreeze in your car. Such substances are designed to prevent freezing in your tissues. However, if they are strong enough to do the job, they will also poison the tissues. This is a relatively young technology being driven by the need to preserve organs for transplant. Progress is being made.

Could this technology be developed to preserve whole bodies? By the use of antifreeze substances that were not toxic, could we lower the temperature of the body without forming ice to the point where all life processes stopped? In other words, could we stop all cellular metabolism by lowering the temperature below freezing without actual ice formation? If so, then we could theoretically cool and thereby suspend the life in the body for an unlimited number of years (if we wanted to). We could preserve the body in the state it was at the time of dying. If a cure was found for whatever killed it, the body could be warmed and healed. We would have achieved our goal of postponing death.

What would such a person feel like after being repaired, warmed up, and revived? The warmed-up person, let's say Mary Jones, would not know about the billion year gap in her life. Reflect that her body was cooled to the point that all motion in every cell stopped. Nothing worked anymore. Nerves in her brain wouldn't transmit. Her life was suspended, or she was dead, or whatever words you want to use. When she woke up, Mary would not be conscious of any event that took place while she was frozen. She would feel exactly the way she did at the moment that her body temperature dropped and her life was suspended. She would know nothing about things that happened during the billion years during which she was effectively dead. When she woke up, Mary would be ready to resume life based on what she remembered of her old life before the Big Gap. Her life span would have been extended by a billion years, but she would wonder what you were talking about if you told her that.

In the pages of this chapter, we have talked about several methods of postponing death. Some are obvious, others less so. The methods mentioned were the avoidance of disease (a pretty obvious one), the prevention of aging (not yet possible), and the freezing of tissues. So far, the first method (avoidance of disease) has been partly achieved by using vaccines, drugs, and other techniques. The second method (prevention of aging) is only a promise. The third method (freezing) can be done at present only with small groups of cells that stay free of intercellular ice crystals.

Now, are there other known ways to delay death besides the ones that have been mentioned?

Well, I can think of at least one more method that is pretty extreme except possibly for use in a science fiction story. Are you ready for it? It involves speed.

Albert Einstein's extraordinary mind figured out that anything that gains speed gets heavier by gaining mass [11, 12]. Take a ball of a given weight, and throw it. Throw it faster, and it will gain weight. Now really wind up, give it all you've got, and it will get even heavier. Strange but true. The increase in mass will hardly be noticeable until the ball gets near the speed of light, which is one hundred and eighty-six thousand miles per second (how is your pitching arm?). At 90 percent of that speed, or one hundred and sixty-seven thousand miles per second, the increase in mass will start to be very noticeable. If the ball gets to the speed of light, it will be as heavy as it can get, which will be infinitely heavy. It will have infinite mass. It can get no heavier.

What's this got to do with postponing death? Simply this.

If your ball that is flying through the air at close to the speed of light has almost infinite mass, then there is no way it can be deflected from its path. It is too heavy and has too much momentum. To change its course would be like you or me pushing on the sun to try to move it. Ridiculous!

Now we come to the part where we delay death. Instead of a ball, imagine a human body hurtling through space at close to the speed of light. Like the ball it would become infinitely massive at this speed. Are you still with me? Not only the body, but also every cell in the body would have this tremendous weight. Every particle in every cell would have infinite mass. What would happen? Presumably the metabolic chemistry in each cell would stop just like it did when we froze a cell. Life would stop, aging would stop. The life span would be extended by whatever period it took for you to complete your voyage. If you traveled to another star a billion light years away at this extraordinary speed and then stopped, you would be a billion years older, but your body structure would not have changed. It would be the same as it was when the voyage started. Because of their infinite mass and inertia, all the molecules in your body would come to a standstill relative to each other. And yet, when your molecules returned to their normal weight as your body slowed down, you would not even notice any gap in your consciousness. For all you know, there was no gap. As we noted with a frozen body, you would resume life based on the memories of your old life. A person traveling near the speed of light would have no recollection of anything happening during that high-speed journey. If the voyage took a billion years, then death would have been delayed by a billion years because your body wouldn't age during the trip, and your normal life expectancy would resume from that point on. That, I believe, is one of the things that Einstein's Special Theory of Relativity tells us. However, in terms of delaying death, it would appear to have little importance for us in our life today. It seems to have theoretical interest only. It's something that, at the moment, we can enjoy reading about in imaginative science fiction.

THE NECESSITY OF DEATH

Now, let's get back to good old Earth. I have talked about ways of postponing death, some of which are practical and others quite impractical. It is impractical to extend longevity by traveling near the speed of light. On the contrary, it is entirely practical to improve longevity by eradicating disease or altering the aging process. Having made a big issue about delaying death, I now feel compelled do an about turn and point out, as you perhaps already know, that death is necessary and even desirable. Death is absolutely required if life is to continue on Earth. A little reflection will make this appear obvious.

Think of it. If all the individual organisms that have ever been born on Earth had continued to live, living things would have run out of space long ago. If you do the arithmetic, you will be astounded at how the numbers add up when two dividing organisms become four, four become eight, eight become sixteen and so on without stop. The early single-celled microbes that started life on Earth about four billion years ago would have formed a thick layer of grey goo if most of them had not died. These enormous numbers would have been reached early in the history of the world. Living space would run out, food would run out. With all these organisms, the Earth's capacity to sustain life would be overwhelmed. The planet covered with the multiplying grey goo of immortal single cells would find that life would whimper out for lack of food and space.

Fortunately for life on Earth, nature invented death. Death took care of the space and food problem. One form of life eats the other, making space. Age, accidents, and disease decimate the population, creating still more space. Now there is room for newcomers. Dead plants decay and form the soil needed for new generations of plants to grow. Life is cycled and recycled. Death, death, death is the story of life's grand success.

But death is not an inevitable program in the genes of a living cell. Nature did not *have* to program death in living cells. This is apparent when we look at cancer cells in culture. Some lines of cancer cells in dishes live and multiply indefinitely. They do not age, they do not die. Death is not a necessary program in the life of the individual, or even groups of individuals (like groups of cancer cells). It is a required program, however, for the survival of life on Earth as a whole, simply to make room for the newcomers. If there were nothing but immortal multiplying cancer cells living on Earth, they would soon run out of resources to sustain their life.

If the world had originally been populated by single cells that didn't die and didn't *divide,* there would be no space problem but there wouldn't be any diversity either. All life would look the same and do the same thing. We wouldn't have worms, insects, fish, dogs, or humans. There would be no diversity of life forms. Here is why.

According to the current theory of evolution, the interesting mix of creatures we have in the world is made possible by random changes in the DNA of genetic cells. This genetic DNA is the DNA in eggs and sperm that forms new individuals. The random DNA changes (called mutations) result in changes to the body. These changes add up over generations, but generally accumulate so slowly that it took three billion years for single-celled microbes to change into the multi-celled creatures [13, 14] such as dogs and people we see today. If there had been no death among the early single-celled creatures, they would have run out of space and food and become extinct, long before such radical changes in DNA might occur. There would be no worms, fish, nor humans. There would be no time for a significant number of DNA mutations to take place because this usually requires many, many generations. Without death, there would be no food and space to sustain all these generations. There would be no animal and plant diversity. Death, and death alone, has made room in the world for life to live and acquire the mutations that eventually changed single cell creatures into us.

TICKING TIME BOMB

And yet, humans are a ticking bomb that may ultimately destroy much of their own world, including themselves. The cycle of life and death will very likely change because of humans. Before humans arrived on this green planet, everything apparently went along in a self-regulating way. The rule was that the fittest survived, and Mother Nature seemed satisfied with that. Now Mother Nature has produced a new species, mankind, and mankind seems about to intervene in this game of life in a big way.

Humans would now like to be in charge of their own evolution. After three million years or so of evolution without human intervention, along we come and are now trying to manipulate the arrangement of genes. Humans have finally acquired the means to be the boss of evolution, or at least, try to be. They have found out, at last, how to manipulate the DNA in their cells. This, many would agree, is an extraordinary event. It is a milestone in evolution. Think about it. Humans can make changes in the span of days or weeks in living bodies that it took nature, using the snail-like process of natural evolution, millions, even billions of years to do. Humans can delete genes, can splice in genes, can change the way our bodies are built and our brains think. They have found the means to do this. Oops! What if these humans, with their new-found knowledge and tools, goof?

Well, humans have arrived at the point where they can unwittingly cause the death of their own species. This capability is only a recent achievement, if you can call it that. As you know, species come and go by the millions [15-17] but there has never been anything quite like the human species. Evolution has finally produced this special breed that, unlike any other, can now deliberately destroy itself.

How could the human species do this? Literally wipe itself out? I guess you know the answer as well as I do. Some ill-planned bioengineering experiments might do the trick. Fiddle around with DNA, and perhaps open a Pandora's box of unexpected, unwelcome sequelae. Or maybe create intelligent, self-replicating robots that decide to use humans for their own purposes before eliminating them. Poor smart, dumb humans. These are possibilities for the future that start out well-intended but could end in disaster for mankind.

Then, of course, we are quite capable right now of extinguishing the human race with the means we have at hand. I am talking about our familiar stockpiles of nuclear, biological, and chemical devices. For example, a war could escalate out of control beyond anything we have seen before. Not even close to previous wars. Such a war could come near to killing off the human race because the whole surface of the globe might be rendered uninhabitable by radioactive fallout, disease, famine, and anarchy. A scenario we fervently hope and optimistically expect to avoid.

Death, as always, has the final say. We can argue with it for a while. We can have a pact with the Grim Reaper, we may learn how to postpone his visit for hundreds or thousands of years or more, but eventually he will knock on our door and remove life from our body. Will this be the end of us? When he finally harvests our body, will that be the end of our existence?

Not according to the scriptures, as you know, and not according to my Saved Consciousness Hypothesis. The Saved Consciousness Hypothesis, as explained in chapter 2, says that we will continue to be conscious after death. Our existence will not be terminated. The Grim Reaper will, in spite of all our struggles, eventually take our physical body, but not our memory and consciousness. That is off limits to him, and that is our great consolation. The Hypothesis predicts that, after death, we will be able to relive the complete consciousness of our past, and interact again with our past environment, and the people and other living things that we have grown to love. The Hypothesis, as you know, does not go so far as to predict a new, unlived life in a new environment after death. There is simply no knowledge of such a thing, but that doesn't mean to say that it doesn't exist. Its existence must presently be confined to the realm of guesswork or faith in the supernatural.

At this point, I think I owe it to my readers to examine the Saved Consciousness Hypothesis in greater detail than we have so far. It was introduced to the Reader in Chapter 2 in a general manner. Please join me now in the upcoming chapter if you are interested in a closer scrutiny of this fascinating possibility.

REFERENCES

1. B. L. Strehler, *Time, Cells, and Aging* (2nd Edition), Academic Press, New York, 1977.
2. E. V. Cowdry, *Problems of Aging* (3rd Edition), Williams & Wilkins, Baltimore, 1952.
3. A. Comfort, *Ageing: The Biology of Senescence,* Holt, Rinehart, Winston, New York, 1964.
4. J. D. Watson and F. H. C. Crick, Genetical Implications of the Structure of Deoxyribonucleic Acid, *Nature, 177,* p. 964. 1953.
5. K. Brown, The Human Genome Business Today, *Scientific American,* pp. 50-55, July 2000.
6. D. R. Marshak, R. L. Gardner, and D. Gottlieb *Stem Cell Biology,* Cold Spring Harbor Laboratory Press, New York, 2001.
7. B. Joy, *Why The Future Doesn't Need Us,* Wired magazine, archive 8.04, April 2000.
8. R. Kurzweil, Will my PC Be Smarter Than I Am? *Time Magazine,* pp. 52-54, June 19, 2000.
9. K. E. Drexler, *Engines of Creation,* Anchor Press/Doubleday, New York 1990.
10. K. B. Storey and J. M. Storey, Frozen and Alive, *Scientific American,* pp. 92-97, December 1990.
11. L. Barnett, *The Universe and Dr. Einstein,* Time Inc. Book Division, New York, pp. 51-55, 1957.
12. D. Bodanis, $E = mc^2$, Walker, New York, pp. 73-83, 2000.
13. S. J. Gould, The Evolution of Life on the Earth, *Scientific American,* pp. 84-91, October 1994.
14. J. S. Levinton, The Big Bang of Animal Evolution, *Scientific American,* pp. 84-91, November 1992.
15. E. O. Wilson, Vanishing Before Our Eyes, *Time* Special Edition, pp. 29-34, Spring 2000.

16. R. Leaky, Extinction Past and Present, *Time* Special Edition, p. 35, Spring 2000.
17. R. M. May, How Many Species Inhabit the Earth, *Scientific American*, pp. 42-48, October 1992.

CHAPTER 5

The Elimination of Death

We have looked in the last two chapters at the nature of death and the postponement of death. Now let's talk about the complete elimination of death. That is to say, no death, period. Let's think at this point of an everlasting life, the continuation of our consciousness into the indefinite future, you and I and everyone else lasting forever. I am talking here about our consciousness, our sense of self surviving the body. As we know, our body eventually stops living. This has been examined in the last two chapters. Our consciousness, on the other hand, is information that, perhaps, is not lost. My Saved Consciousness Hypothesis, as you know, states that it is continuously recorded and preserved in subatomic space.

What significance this may have for the universe at large I have no idea. Why are we here? Is the Universe better off, worse off, or changed in any important way if our existence is eternal or not? What difference does it make to the cosmos whether or not our consciousness ends when the body dies? I don't think anybody on Earth knows anything about a master plan for the universe. Maybe we don't want to know. For the present, let's simply ask the question: do we exist forever? Is that what actually happens, or does our consciousness, our sense of personal identity, simply snuff out when we die? Does it disappear as though it never existed? I intend to go into this matter in the present chapter which forms a sequel to chapter 2.

The scriptures say no, we are not snuffed out, that our "soul" exists forever. This dogma is the meat and potatoes of most religions [1]. The book you are holding does not attempt to dispute such a view. In fact, it supports it. It supports the continuation of our individual identity. But it does something else. It attempts to show a mechanism by which eternal existence may come about. It examines a chain of possible events that may be happening even as we speak to preserve consciousness beyond death.

In chapter 2 we looked at the possibility of nature moving a replica of consciousness voltages and memory patterns from the brain to a more permanent location, namely, very small regions between and within atoms referred to as subatomic space. It was suggested that this transfer was taking place on an ongoing basis during our lives, but no mechanism was proposed by which the transfer might be done. I talked in a general way about radio (electromagnetic) waves and how we use them in our daily lives to transmit all sorts of information. In chapter 2, I did not hazard a guess as to *how* these waves may be involved in the transfer of consciousness and its preservation in another location. I thought I would leave that for another chapter. Well, we have come to that other chapter and will now get to it. By what physical method does our consciousness get from here to there? How does memory and consciousness get from the brain to a subatomic field and become regenerated there so we live again? Could such a thing happen?

Again I am going to point, as I did in chapter 2, to something we commonly do in our everyday lives. This, I think, will serve as a useful analogy for the transfer and storage of consciousness. What we do is create data (such as music) at one place, transmit it to another place electronically, and record it at this other place. This is actually being done billions and billions of times a day. In other words, information is being electronically transmitted from one place to another and then stored at the new location. When it gets there, it can be *retrieved*. That is the important point. The original music, or data, can be regenerated. It is not lost. A duplicate has been made. If you have made a good recording, if your duplicate is faithful, then you will have the equivalent of the original and you will not be able to tell the difference from the original.

This same principle, at least theoretically, is possibly being used to transmit and record our consciousness as we go through life, and to make it available for regeneration after the death of the brain. Certainly this would seem like a strange idea but, I suggest, it merits examination. How could it take place?

THE FINAL COMMON PATHWAY

Let us, you and I, walk through the door of that recording studio down the street and see what the sound engineers are doing. We will compare what is happening in the studio when the signals from the numerous microphones are mixed down to a final common pathway in the mixing console, to what is happening in a person's brain when that person receives signals from the outside world and mixes them down to the proposed final common pathway in the brain. The analogy is broad but I think will serve to relate the unfamiliar idea of mixing down brain signals to the more familiar one of mixing down music.

Let's go. We walk into the studio where we see a group of musicians blowing their horns and scraping on their violins, cellos, and so on. The blowing and scraping causes the air to vibrate, and these vibrations push and pull on the diaphragms of microphones placed around the room. This is the picture of the recording studio that will be convenient to keep in mind as we proceed. So far, so good?

Now, if we want to compare these goings on to what happens in the brain, we must first look for the microphones or their facsimiles that are connected to the brain and serve to transmit the various signals from the external world to the brain. The microphones in this case are the sense organs. You know what the human sense organs are [2]. To refresh your memory, they are the eyes, ears, tongue, nose, and senses in the skin for touch, pressure, temperature, and pain, all of which keep our consciousness in touch with part of what's going on in the world external to the brain. When these sense organs, the brain's microphones, are hit by outside signals such as vibrating air, light, or whatever they are sensitive to, they transmit the signals in the same manner that microphones in the studio do. They send the signals to the brain giving information about the outside world, whether it is the sight of a bird flying by, the sound of its song, or feel of the bird if it should land on your finger.

Okay. We must look now at how these signals are transmitted. In the studio, each microphone sends its signal by a wire [3, pp. 61-155]. The sense organs, however, do not use wires, but they use something similar. They use nerves, which do the same thing. Each sense organ sends its signal to the brain by a nerve. The signal in both cases is electrical. It works like this:

In the studio, the microphones change the sound vibrations in the air to electric voltages in a wire. The wire from each microphone sends its voltage wave to a studio mixing console that combines the voltages into one single wave [3, pp. 461-519]. This is important. No longer do we have many individual waves from the various microphones and instruments, but one wave representing them all. Do you believe me? It's true. In other words, the sounds from the different microphones get mixed together into one sound, one wave, the sound of the whole orchestra. If we were to connect the output or final common pathway of the mixing console to an oscilloscope (an instrument that can show voltages), we would see on the oscilloscope screen that the different waves from the various microphones have all combined to form a single wave visible now as one lone wiggly line on the screen.

It's not easy to imagine that the sound of a whole orchestra, a sound that is complex and has a very detailed texture, could be completely contained in one wiggly voltage wave. For proof, just plug the voltage wave, suitably amplified, into a loudspeaker, and you will hear the whole orchestra in all its detail. Those studio technicians have turned sound into measurable electricity and back into sound again. I am impressed!

How is all this stuff going on in the studio comparable to what goes on in the brain? Let me explain.

The brain is analogous to the studio-mixing console. The brain is the ultimate mixer, putting the studio mixer to shame with its stunning combining abilities. It is able to combine together the various signals from all the different senses and, according to the Saved Consciousness Hypothesis, send them as one voltage wave in what may be referred to as a final common voltage pathway. I will call it the "objective" voltage wave of consciousness as a matter of convenience. I use the word "objective" because the final common voltage pathway is potentially measurable in a physical way like the voltage output of the studio-mixing console. Instead of converting the voltage into something that can be heard as music over a loudspeaker, the brain converts the combined voltages of all the senses and memory into consciousness. That is what I tentatively believe. In time, this will be proved, or disproved.

Where are we? Let's try to keep things clear by summarizing. At the risk of being monotonously repetitive, let me go back. In the studio, the microphones send their signal fluctuations along wires. This, of course, is not what happens in the human. As you know, the human sense organs send signal fluctuations ("action potentials") along nerves instead of wires. In both cases, the signals consist of fluctuations of electricity. The proof of this is that these voltage fluctuations, whether in a wire or in a nerve, can be seen in the form of voltage waves on the screen of an oscilloscope which is a common electronic instrument commonly used to plot electrical changes.

Okay. I trust you're with me. So far, we are looking at voltage fluctuations in a studio wire on the one hand, and in a human nerve on the other. Let's follow these voltage fluctuations to see where they go.

In the recording studio, they go from the microphones to a mixing console whose main job is to blend together the sounds of the different musical instruments. Recall that these sounds have been converted into electricity. The mixing console combines the air vibrations and resulting voltage wave of each instrument to produce a single voltage wave with its own brand new shape that is a blend of all the separate waves. The new wiggly wave contains the sound of all the instruments blended together and is different from the individual waves that formed it. In other words, the unique waveform of the trumpet, the special wave form of the violin, the distinct wave form of the solo singer, all merge together in a final common pathway in the mixer which is a new, single wave with its own shape, the result of many waves combined to form one. The blended sound of the whole orchestra has been captured in one single wiggly line. The wiggles are the electricity fluctuations in a wire. Connect this wire to a loudspeaker and lo! you will hear the sound of the entire orchestra. The various sounds have been mixed to a final common pathway forming one sound.

Now, are you ready for the brain? This long-winded story about what goes on in a studio-mixing console is to show, by analogy, what may be going on in the brain. Please note that the interpretation is mine, and has not been confirmed.

The brain is a mixer. As I have noted, the voltage fluctuations in nerves from our five senses go to the brain to be mixed down to a final common pathway that may be called "objective" consciousness. The voltages of consciousness are potentially measurable.

Now comes a new level of complexity. The final common pathway (objective consciousness) branches and goes to two networks in the brain (this has to be tested by future research). One network may be called (for lack of a better name) a "subjective" black box. The subjective black box consists of nerves and their connections receiving one of the branches of the final common pathway. This gives us our subjective sense of consciousness in life. The place receiving the other branch of the final common pathway is the subatomic space of the brain that is within and between the atoms making up the substance of the brain. This is where the objective consciousness wave is recorded and preserved.

Let's start with the subjective black box that is located in the brain and which is postulated to consist of some part of the brain's nerve networks. I say "postulated" because, when I talk about a subjective black box, I am dealing with an idea, not a demonstrable fact.

The part of the objective wave that goes into the subjective black box is a physical, tangible, measurable thing. It is processed and transformed in the alleged subjective box into the thing we find so hard to describe and that we all recognize as a personal awareness of our existence. It is what we refer to as I, or me. This is what the subjective black box does. It is able to process the objective final common pathway of all the brain's networks to give us the subjective impression of consciousness. That's why I call the black box a "subjective" box. Our feeling of self-awareness is the result of the objective consciousness wave that was obtained from the senses and memory and is processed in the brain's so-called subjective black box. In other words, the subjective black box in the brain is able to process the combined impulses of the sensory and memory nerves to give the subjective impression of consciousness. If you are skeptical, you are rightly so. How is the single, measurable, objective wave manipulated in the circuits of the subjective black box to produce subjective consciousness?

Ah, wouldn't we like to know! It is impossible to say at this time. We do know from experience that our subjective consciousness is personal, private, and internal. It is not shared with other people as a common resource. The objective nerve impulses coming from both the senses and memory must be converted into subjective awareness at some location or locations in the brain that I have called, for convenience, the subjective black box and am obliged to leave it at that.

People have been trying to paint a picture of consciousness for thousands of years and the picture is still not clear. Consciousness has been talked about in terms of self, identity, ego, id, psyche, soul, spirit, and so on. These are all words relating, I think, to the subjective sense we have of ourselves. They are abstract, fuzzy, and inadequate. They tell us nothing about the physics, chemistry, and electricity of consciousness. What seems certain, however, is that our awareness of ourselves in relation to our environment is built up by voltage changes that take place in the nerves leading from our sense organs to the brain. We would like to trace the paths of these voltage changes after they enter the brain to see where they go, and to find out how they interact with each other to produce consciousness. Do they mix down to a final common pathway of consciousness as I propose? The unraveling of the brain networks and their relation to consciousness is the brain's untold story and, as you might imagine, the subject of ongoing investigation. The subject comes under the heading of cognitive neuroscience.

Please let me emphasize once again that my proposal of a final common pathway for consciousness is purely hypothetical. It does not in any way represent an established consensus. It is merely what seems to me a reasonable and useful hypothesis for consciousness. It builds on the known fact that waves representing voltage changes can be superposed upon one another to form a single composite wave. We saw this when we mixed the many sound waves of individual instruments in a studio to form the single sound wave of a whole orchestra. However, it is speculation to say that there is a single composite wave in the brain that is synonymous with consciousness. Yet it makes sense, at least to me. If it is a fact, then the composite wave should be accessible for measurement with an oscilloscope. In other words, this part of the

Saved Consciousness Hypothesis should be testable. We will look at the idea of testing for a final common pathway of consciousness a little later in this chapter.

It should help us to understand what's involved in mixing down several inputs to a final common pathway if we look now in slightly more detail at the mixers: first the mixing console in the recording studio, then the brain which is the human mixing console involved in consciousness (Appendix III).

The studio mixer, as we have seen, merges incoming signals from different microphones into one wave. Brass, woodwinds, strings, and so on. But merging the signals is not all that the mixer does. It also modifies, or changes, the signals. The studio mixer has a network of connections to and from various devices that, for simplification, we will call effects boxes. These effects boxes can modify any signal (voltage) that is sent to them. They can change the sound of a musical instrument. Depending on how fancy the mixer is, and how much you pay for it, these effects boxes can change a sound by amplifying it, attenuating it, changing pitch, adding time delay, adding reverberation, changing phase, limiting, compressing, and so on [3, pp. 205-245, 247-297, 299-329]. These effects boxes change the sound of the music in a way the operator of the mixing console believes will be more pleasing to the listener, or at least to his boss, the producer. Ultimately, all voltage pathways in the mixer converge to a final common pathway, that is to say, a single waveform that comes out of the mixer's main output and can be sent to a loudspeaker or to a recording machine. That's what a studio mixing console is for and can do.

Now, what about the brain that is surely the ultimate mixer? The brain has an almost unlimited network of nerve connections with countless effects boxes to which they can shuttle signals back and forth and have them modified. The signals (voltages) coming from the five senses and from the brain's memory are routed, re-routed, and routed again through this maze of nerve networks. Are you getting dizzy? Unlike the studio mixer whose relatively few connections are known and can all be drawn in a diagram like a road map, nobody has much of a clue about the connections in the brain and how they should be drawn. The connections number in the trillions. We only have a very rough idea of the general overall geography of these connections [4]. As mentioned before, if we compare a map of the brain to a map of the world, we have an idea in the brain where the continents may be located, but know little about the countries, states, provinces, cities, streets, lanes, and what goes on in them.

This lack of knowledge about the pathways of the brain is somewhat intimidating to someone that wants to understand consciousness.

How can one possibly comprehend the inner workings of such a complex piece of biological machinery without at least having a decent road map? How does one start to unravel the exquisite detail of trillions of interwoven nerve branches in a search for consciousness? How do we objectively test for consciousness?

Every journey has to have a first step, and the first step in this case is to look at different parts of the brain in a living person to see how they change with thought. For example, thought can be indicated by regions of heightened neural activity, and these in turn may be identified by increases in blood flow and blood oxygen to those regions. In the last twenty-five years or so, we have developed ways to look at these [5, 6].

Example 1. PET (positron emission tomography). Here, radioactively labeled water is injected into the vein of a subject. The radioactive water gives off particles called positrons that react with electrons to produce detectable gamma rays. These gamma rays can be used to form an image of blood flow in the brain. When the subject does different things such as reading, listening, or talking, the blood flow increases in those regions of the brain involved with that particular activity, and we get an idea of what part of the brain is being used for a specific task.

Example 2. fMRI (functional magnetic resonance imaging). This technique uses a magnetic field to detect an increase in blood oxygen wherever there is a region of increased brain activity. Using this method, the regions of brain activity can be pinned down to within a couple of millimeters, and this is an improvement in localization over PET.

Example 3. MEG (magnetoencephalography). Here we do not use changes in blood flow or blood oxygen to show increased brain activity, but instead, we pick up magnetic fields generated by neuronal activity in the active regions. However, MEG (like all present forms of encephalography) is not as good at pinpointing the active region as PET or especially fMRI. Its advantage is that, unlike PET and fMRI, it responds instantly to the nerve activity. There is no time lag involved. You know what is going on, and you know it now.

Would any of these methods of localizing brain activity be useful in mapping the networks of nerve fibers that produce consciousness? Yes. They might be used as a rough guide indicating some likely places to look. Unfortunately, no single one of the above methods, or any combination of them, would be able to select a consciousness wave from all the other electrical activity that is going on. They lack the required precision. The smallest regions of the brain that the above techniques can deal with are measured in millimeters, a size visible to the naked eye. We must get smaller than this. To detect and follow the alleged neural pathways that form consciousness, it may be necessary to use microscopic electrodes inserted into the brain tissue of a conscious human. These might give the required precision to locate consciousness pathways. The subject, who would feel no pain, might readily agree to submit to this procedure during routine brain surgery. The experimental scientist might work in tandem with the operating surgeon. The search by the scientist would be for the alleged final common pathway of consciousness. The painstaking exercise of matching voltage readings with thought processes and mapping the connections would involve many procedural refinements and much experimentation on the human animal. According to neuroscientist N. K. Logothetist, only a tiny fraction of neurons seem to be plausible candidates for what physiologists call the "neural correlate" of conscious perception. He states that learning more about the locations of, and connections between, neurons that correlate with conscious experience will tell us more about how the brain generates awareness [7-10]. That is to say, see which neurons are activated by thinking. This is pie in the sky at the moment, but what a prize if the outcome was successful! We would have the final location of a voltage wave that correlates with thought. That is to say, we would know which nerves were involved.

The challenge of finding a consciousness wave may seem somewhat overwhelming except for a single simplifying factor that should give some comfort to the investigator: we appear to be dealing with nothing more complicated than electricity in nerves. We wish to find out how the voltages in the brain are affected by the effects boxes they pass through, and what shape the alleged final wiggly waveform might take. It is perhaps reassuring to the investigator to know that the complex sound of a symphony can be obtained from a single wiggly wave in a wire. I postulate that the complex voltages of consciousness likewise can be measured as a single waveform.

What role does memory play in this picture of consciousness? It is necessary for the memory to feed into, and form part of, this waveform or final common pathway of consciousness. Memory is a vital component of consciousness because the five senses alone are not enough to create self-awareness. According to J. Huttenlocher, a professor of psychology at the University of Chicago, "there's almost nothing you do, from perception to thinking, that doesn't draw continuously on your memory" [11, p. 42]. M. D. Lemonick, science writer, notes: "Without a memory of what's been said, none of what you are now reading makes the slightest sense. The same is true for our lives as a whole. Memory provides personal context, a past and present and a frame for the future" [12, p. 42].

As you know, I have been holding forth a great deal about "voltages" and "final common pathways" in this chapter. Are you getting a bit tired of hearing about them? Presumably you picked up this book because you wanted to read about life after death, not voltages. I'm sorry, but it seems we can't avoid voltages. As distasteful as voltages may be to you, I believe that consciousness is exclusively about voltages and so is life after death. Consciousness *is* voltages. It's as simple as that. The brain and consciousness and the question of life after death, according to the author's Saved Consciousness Hypothesis, is all about voltages, so I must continue to talk about them. If you are waiting for the life after death part of this chapter, I assure you it's coming soon.

Voltage fluctuations play a part in almost everything we do today, from turning on the lights to driving cars, talking on telephones, and watching television. That's not all. The many forms of life, from plants to humans and the cells of which they are composed, work by voltage fluctuations inside and outside the cells. Also, the heavens are filled with voltage changes as anyone can see who has watched the northern lights. My Hypothesis postulates that voltage changes play an essential part in life after death. They are vital to preserving Aunt Dorothy after the grave.

Let me now try to explain how this may work. I will suggest to you a possible mechanism for the transfer of consciousness from the brain to a separate domain that is not of flesh and blood. To put the last piece of the puzzle in place, first please let me say just a word about tape recorders [3, pp. 379-422] because these form a good and more familiar analogy (to some) for the principles involved. We are still talking about consciousness transfer, and playback after death.

In the imaginary tour of a recording studio that we took earlier in this chapter, we did not see any recording machine at work. I omitted to insert one. Let me now correct that oversight by putting a magnetic tape recorder in the studio. The engineers connect the tape recorder to the mixing console, which delivers to it the music being played by the musicians. The mixing console is sending out a final wiggly waveform of that music to the tape recorder. As you remember, this single wiggly wave on a wire contains the music of the whole orchestra, and that is what is recorded.

How? You may remember from high school physics (sorry to remind you of school) that voltage wiggles in a wire create a corresponding wiggly magnetic field around them. Our wavy voltage from the mixer goes into the recording head of the tape machine (a coil of wire) and creates a corresponding wavy magnetic field around the recording head. Now, if you drag a tape with metal particles on it across the recording head, what happens? The tiny metal particles are magnetized by the magnetic field of the recording head and take up new positions on the tape. That's what the recording head does. Result? The tape now contains a permanent record of the music voltages. Proof? Draw the tape across the *playback* head of the tape recorder (another coil of wire), and wow! The voltage wave (there we go again!) that was fed into the tape is now returned to you, courtesy of the magnetized particles. Feed these voltages from the moving tape to a loudspeaker and you will recreate the original music, or vibrations in the air, that was played by the musicians in the first place (or very close to it). You transmitted the original voltages from mixing console to tape, then regenerated them when the tape was played back. In a three-step process, you were able to transmit information, store it, then regenerate it. That, I postulate, is what the brain does with consciousness. It is transmitted and stored during life, then regenerated after death.

Now, there are a lot of things left hanging here. Do you want to pause for a beer, cup of coffee, or run out of the room screaming? I hope you come back, because we have a little way to go. You may think my idea is off the wall, but with a little patience and interest, I'm sure you will at least understand it. We still have to see how all this may relate to post mortem existence.

TRANSFER AND PLAYBACK

How is it possible for consciousness to get from the brain to a subatomic quantum field where, according to the Saved Consciousness Hypothesis, it leaves a permanent record that is capable of being regenerated into the real thing? How can we live our life again after death? Recall that the Saved Consciousness Hypothesis postulates a continuous transfer of consciousness and memory throughout life, not just at the time of death. How does this transfer take place? How does Nature pull it off? And how is it regenerated so that we are put back into our former life?

The mechanism I propose is based on the following concepts.

Earlier in this chapter, I proposed that the objective wave, or final common pathway, of consciousness splits and goes to two destinations. One destination is the subjective box consisting of nerve networks in the brain. The second destination (and now we are in new territory) is the subatomic space in the brain (the space within and between all atoms). It is postulated that the voltages of the objective wave exert an electromagnetic field in this subatomic space, and this "field effect" becomes permanently embedded there. How? That is the big question. One might postulate the existence of monopoles, solitons, or other "knots" in the subatomic field [13, 14] that reconfigure the space field to correspond to the magnetic field of the final common pathway. The field is analogous to the metal particles on magnetic recording tape. If such were the case, we would now have all the voltage numbers of the consciousness wave embedded in space. The very voltages that formed the final common pathway in the brain would be recorded in subatomic space, available for regeneration or "playback." Is this what actually happens? Who knows? My point is that, by this or some other mechanism, the electromagnetic voltages of consciousness do get permanently recorded in subatomic space and are available for playback.

Now, I believe there is something else important to think about in connection with transferring consciousness to space, and that is the motion of the brain through space. The brain is moving quickly through space, and this complicates the transfer. Let me explain.

Have you ever stopped to think how well traveled your brain is? You might be surprised. Consider this. You and your brain move from room to room, city to city, country to country. You move with the surface of the Earth as it turns. You move through space with the Earth as it orbits the Sun, with the Sun as it shifts its position in the Milky Way, with the Milky Way as it does cart-wheels in space and, in addition, speeds away from other galaxies. Your brain is weaving a crazy zig-zag course through space even though you may not realize it. And here is the point I wish to make: your brain passes through all this space like a sieve leaving the space behind. The space and its force fields stay in one place while the brain moves through it.

Think about this as an analogy. The brain and its atoms may be compared to a piece of wire mesh that moves through space leaving the space behind. The mesh moves, but the space is fixed and filters through the mesh. If this space field contains the consciousness voltages transferred to it by the brain, then these too are left behind. Think of the brain reeling out voltages in space as though it were a boat reeling out fishing line as it moves through the water. Since the consciousness voltages are reeled out in an ongoing way throughout life, the brain leaves an uninterrupted trail of consciousness voltages in space wherever it goes. The consciousness wave trails the moving brain like the breadcrumbs that marked Hansel and Gretel's trail in the forest. The brain lays down a curving trail in the sky perhaps trillions of miles long consisting of voltage numbers rather than bread crumbs. That is a postulate of the Saved Consciousness Hypothesis.

Now comes the question of power.

"Hold on," you say, "How could the brain develop enough power to leave a permanent electromagnetic recording a trillion miles long?"

Well, a part of the answer to this question may lie in the smallness of the subatomic volume. The amount of power needed to leave a trace voltage signal in a subatomic volume of space might be close to zero. As long as the brain continues to work and be nourished by glucose and oxygen (which it is, of course, during life), then there is plenty of power to radiate its electromagnetic voltages to subatomic space.

There is another source of power besides that which the brain produces by its metabolic activity, and that has to do with the brain's motion. The brain is moving through space at a zillion miles per hour. But the space field through which the motion is taking place is, as we have noted, fixed. One thing is moving, the other is not. This relative difference in motion involving electrical charges is, according to Maxwell's equations concerning electromagnetism, a potential source of unlimited power for embedding the ongoing consciousness voltages wherever the brain travels.

Now, the question of playback. Of what good is recorded consciousness unless it gets played back?

Playback or regeneration of the embedded consciousness voltages after death is the way that the life we live can potentially be recycled or lived again. But playback requires energy. At this point, the brain is dead, and so the energy cannot come from it. The voltage numbers are stuck in cold, empty space. Where does the energy come from to regenerate those voltages? Where in empty space is there a source of energy? Do we have a problem here?

I don't think so. Actually, the so-called empty space is not really empty. It is pregnant with force fields that can reach such energetic intensity that they can create new particles, such as electrons and positrons, which in fact come fleetingly into existence and then annihilate each other [15, 16]. Thus, one can suggest that there is sufficient "vacuum energy" available in space to regenerate and amplify the voltage numbers embedded in its subatomic field. Power is no problem.

Given this scenario, we are led next to another obvious question. How would the playback, which only produces voltage fluctuations, reproduce the subjective feeling of consciousness in space?

In the brain, you may recall, I postulated a so-called subjective black box that processes the objective voltage wave and turns it into the subjective consciousness we feel and recognize as ourselves. But we are no longer dealing with the brain here. It's dead. We are dealing with its final common voltage pattern embedded in subatomic space. How can the feeling of identity and self-awareness be produced in this non-brain environment? We have the voltage wave recorded there, but where is the subjective box that can transform it into subjective consciousness? We need a subjective box.

I can only suggest that there must exist in the force fields of space something analogous to the *subjective* black box in the brain. This black box in space would, of course, be built in a different way and with different materials [17] than it was in the brain, but nevertheless be designed to process the voltage numbers in space into subjective consciousness. As in the brain, the objective consciousness wave that was formed originally by the senses and the memory and recorded in subatomic space reaches the subjective box in space, and subjective consciousness is experienced. In other words, this new processing unit (subjective black box) in space would accept the regenerated objective voltages of consciousness and, like the brain, create from them the impression of self-awareness. If God or nature is able to build a subjective consciousness box using the macroscopic materials of the brain, then (according to the Saved Consciousness Hypothesis) God or nature is also capable of constructing a box in space that will do the same thing using different materials. D. J. Chalmers has stated that physical systems with the same abstract organization will give rise to the same kind of conscious experience, no matter what they are made of [17]. That is to say, we may use a different place and different building blocks, but the same consciousness experience will result. You may feel that this is a big bite to chew on, but I believe it is theoretically conceivable. It seems consistent with the belief of physicists like Gerard t'Hooft (cited earlier in chapter 2) that no information can be lost.

As a side issue, it is intriguing to conjecture that some dead person's regenerated voltages from subatomic quantum space, suitably amplified, might theoretically be fed directly to the subjective box in your brain in this life, and that would result in the rather interesting situation of someone else's past consciousness being present in your brain!

When our consciousness voltage numbers are relocated, how safe are they? How permanent are they? What would happen to the subatomic space in your brain containing your consciousness wave if your brain gets blown up?

As I see it, the embedded voltages are perfectly safe. Space everywhere seems to be a permanent fixture, so the destruction of the brain would have no effect on this subatomic space or on someone's consciousness embedded in its force field. The voltage wave of consciousness would remain undisturbed regardless of what happened to the brain. For example, you can set off an explosion in space, but force fields (gravity, for example) remain undisturbed. For this reason, I reason that our past consciousness is not lost. Our identity, and the life that we lived, can be regenerated from the voltage numbers permanently retained in space. The very events that gave us consciousness for the first time during life can be regenerated. We can experience again everything that we experienced during our first life because we are dealing with exactly the same consciousness wave that went through our brain in the first place. Why should we feel any different? It is postulated that all events would be available for complete regeneration. Nothing lost, no one forgotten, no event from the past omitted. We start the same life over again. The people we knew would be the same, the things we liked to do would be there to do again in exactly the same way. We would not simply be watching like an outsider looking at a movie, but we would be in the movie, doing these things, interacting with these people, feeling the same pleasure and pain that we felt the first time around.

Likely story, you may say. Where is the truth in any of this? What kind of a speculative goose-chase is this author trying to take me on?

The question is valid.

It goes without saying that the hypothesis outlined above is for the most part speculative. Speculation, nevertheless, cannot be tossed aside as worthless if it is extrapolated from fact. I believe that the electromagnetic principles of this hypothesis are extrapolated from fact. Whether or not there is a final common pathway of consciousness in the brain, and whether it is recorded in subatomic space, has definitely not been determined. That is a field of investigation, it seems to me, that may hold some allure for future researchers. According to physicist Freeman Dyson, a hypothesis is "useful only insofar as it may suggest new experiments" [18].

At this point, may I suggest that the Reader try another little thought experiment, if his or her brain is not already twisted into a pretzel. This time it will be to compare recycling consciousness before death with recycling consciousness after death. This will become clear in the two examples that follow. Both examples will be imaginary.

BEFORE DEATH: Suppose you are six years old and enjoying your birthday party. Your mother, seeing what a good time you're having, strings a long wire between your brain and a recording machine (a perfectly ordinary one like a Sony cassette recorder) and records your consciousness wave during the whole party. She places the record on a shelf where you come across it many years later and recognize it from the label: "Birthday party, 6 years old, consciousness wave." "Ah," you say, "I'd like to experience that birthday party again." Note: the word is "experience," not merely watch or listen.

You put the tape into the cassette machine and hit play. A lot of incomprehensible noise comes out of the loudspeaker. You realize you have made a mistake, for you shouldn't have connected the tape to a loudspeaker. You remedy things by pulling the plug out of the speaker and you connect it, instead, to the subjective consciousness black box in your brain. Now hit the play button. The black box turns the objective consciousness wave with its raw voltages into a feeling of subjective awareness (you have taken the precaution of shutting off the other inputs to your brain's subjective box so you won't get interference). Hey! You are experiencing your sixth birthday party again, eating the same ice cream, playing with the same friends. That is because the consciousness wave that your mother was smart enough to record on your sixth birthday is being experienced by your living brain *again*. Why should you feel any different than you did the first time? You don't.

The record comes to an end, you put all switches back to their normal position, and carry on with your life, swearing that you have just experienced your sixth birthday party. You have actually relived a day in your past simply by playing back a record your mother made of your consciousness wave when you were six years old. The whole scenario, I think, is theoretically do-able but is predicated, of course, on the existence of an objective consciousness wave and a subjective black box in the brain to which you can plug in the tape recorder.

AFTER DEATH: The scene changes. We imagine that there is some kind of new life that you are living after you have died, and that you are seated in your post-mortem living room in subatomic space, feeling lonely for your past life. You go to the shelf and pull out a tape labeled "Birthday party, 6 years old, consciousness wave." You put it on the cassette player at your side and feed the cassette player's output to the subjective black box in space also located beside you. Hit the play button, and lo! You are experiencing your sixth birthday party, living it up again with the ice cream and your pals even though you're dead.

The recording ends, and you go back to the shelf. "Mmm," you muse, "I think I'd like to re-live the day I met my first wife." You select the tape by its label (the record might consist of fixed magnetic monopoles in a charged field) and hit the play button (which might cause relative motion between the monopoles and the field), and you are back meeting your first wife. Note: you are not watching the meeting or hearing the meeting, you are actually living the meeting.

When you have finished re-living the past, you return the recording to the shelf and get on with your new post-mortem life if you have one.

You have, at least, touched base with your former life, a life that was the origin of your identity in death.

End of thought experiment.

It seems obvious from these two imaginary examples that it doesn't matter where or when the consciousness wave is recorded and played back—in ordinary space in real life or in subatomic space after death. A duck is a duck is a duck, and the same applies to a consciousness wave. Wherever and whenever the wave is repeated, then consciousness in a past life will be re-created.

QUESTIONS

The mechanisms outlined above concerning the permanent storage of consciousness and its regeneration after death may strike some readers as feasible. Others may think the mechanisms are unlikely but nevertheless remotely possible, at least in principle. Some readers will, on the other hand, be left holding their sides, regarding the whole scenario as high comedy that wouldn't even qualify for science fiction. Whatever your take may be, it is obvious that a host of questions remain to be answered. Here is one.

How do we get the consciousness wave in the quantum domain to playback? We are not dealing with a tape recorder where playback is easy. With a tape recorder, you just drag the tape across the wire coil in the playback head, and the magnetized particles on the tape give you back your music by regenerating the appropriate voltages. But we're in subatomic quantum space where there are no tape recorders. Where in quantum space are the magnetized particles that were on the tape? There are none. We must look for magnetic patterns other than metal particles. I have postulated magnetized points in this space corresponding to the magnetized particles on a tape. I suggest that these points might be magnetic monopoles or knots in the magnetic field sometimes referred to as solitons [13, 14]. These would serve as playback nodes analogous to metal particles on tape. But there is another problem. We need motion. What moves? One might postulate a charged field moving relative to the fixed magnetized points, thus regenerating the voltages of the embedded wave of consciousness. By analogy to a tape recorder, the tape (embedded wave) would be stationary but the tape head (charged field) would move across it.

We turn to another unanswered question that raises its ugly head: what might be the trigger that starts up subatomic quantum consciousness after death? Whatever the trigger is, why does it wait for death to activate the subatomic consciousness wave? Or does it? Recall that the Saved Consciousness Hypothesis postulates that consciousness and memory are transferred to the subatomic quantum domain in a continuous, ongoing fashion during life. What trigger starts it up again? What is there about the death of the brain that should cause the consciousness embedded in subatomic space to be activated or, as it were, kick in? The transfer of the consciousness wave to subatomic space is postulated to begin with the first moments of conscious life in the womb. What causes these voltages to be regenerated or played back only after death? Why not during life? How is it that we are not living in two places at once? Or are we? The Saved Consciousness Hypothesis offers no answers.

Another question begs for an answer. Are there not other fluctuating voltages in the brain to which the adjacent subatomic space is exposed that could interfere with the embedding of the consciousness wave? In the brain itself, the subatomic space closest to the wave source would receive the strongest radiation, but other waves are also present in the brain. Other voltage waves must occur in the vicinity that are not consciousness waves. After all, the brain is full of electrical activity that can be demonstrated simply by attaching electrodes to the scalp. What is it about the consciousness wave that makes it so special that it is the only wave to get embedded in quantum space? Is it because of special frequency selection in that space? Is it because of the greater amplitude of the consciousness wave which elbows out other waves in the vicinity? These questions remain unanswered.

Here's another puzzle. If the consciousness of every living being, past and present, is embedded in subatomic space, how is the consciousness of one individual separated from another? How is the voltage wave of your consciousness separated from mine? Would they not interfere with each other? Is there intermingling or superposition? As I see it, the answer would be yes, and no. It raises the idea of the superposition of waves, the combining of one wave with another to make a new wave. This, as we have seen, happens when you take the individual waves of many musical instruments and superpose or combine them in a single wave to produce the sound of the orchestra as a whole. Similarly, we can imagine consciousness waves being superposed to give a new and different "sound." This idea might be in accord with certain religions, such as the Hindu belief that, at some point after our death following a long series of re-incarnations, we merge with God (Brahman). In this instance, our consciousness wave would be merged with that of God. If such could be imagined, then God would have an indestructible record of the whole of his changing creation seen from the perspective of his created beings as they witnessed it.

Some more recent philosophers have pondered this question of fusing the consciousness of individuals. For example, John Hick and H. H. Price [19, chapters 14 and 15; 20] envisage a community of centers of consciousness where the memory of each member is telepathically available to all; that is, all memories are shared by a community of "souls." This idea fails to fit with a basic assumption of the Saved Consciousness Hypothesis, which is that the memories and consciousness of all organisms, not just humans, are translocated. If these memories were shared, a human might get a closer feel for a worm's predicament on a fish hook, or a lobster's problem with boiling water. But how could a worm or a lobster, with their limited and specialized experience, make sense out of human memories of, say, a chess game, a history lesson, or a debate in Congress? A comprehensive understanding of a world reconstructed from the memories of all the diverse organisms that have lived in it through time would only be possible, it seems, in the mind of one who was capable of assimilating the individual experiences of each organism from that organism's own point of view. If credit is given to the concept of an omnipotent Creator who could sense the total experience of every creature on Earth, then it may be supposed that He could construct a world in His "mind" that corresponded to the sum-total of all experience. This would be the world that we and our fellow creatures recognize as our own. Whereas the lobster cannot invent mankind's world, nor mankind the lobster's, the Creator might do both.

Life after death is a subject that fascinates humans when they occasionally pause to think about it. Are there any real answers out there? The Saved Consciousness Hypothesis says, maybe. We may not have to rely forever on guesswork, intuition, and scriptural hearsay to provide answers. Science may show sooner or later whether or not nature has prepared a personal existence for living beings after they die.

There is another way, perhaps less appealing, to think about life after death. Inventors, even as we speak, are beavering away in the field of artificial intelligence [21-23]. Some of them dream of downloading the human brain to a robot [24]. What good would that do? Well, if the robot were indestructible, or could be replicated, that would seem to be a way of getting around brain death. The robot's brain might be made indestructible. You and I would be conscious as a robot, not as a human being, and our consciousness would, perhaps, be preserved in a brain that would not perish.

To download consciousness to a robot, it would seem that the consciousness wave must be fed from the human brain to the robot's brain, and the robot's brain must then process these voltage fluctuations to generate subjective consciousness in its own head. I allege that the human brain does this in the networks of its so-called subjective consciousness box. What might go on in this box is a big question. Ongoing research into artificial intelligence may someday shine a light on this enigma. D. Chalmers has noted that, if the precise interactions between our neurons could be duplicated with silicon chips, the same conscious experience would arise [17].

Downloading the human brain to a robot might give us the best of two worlds: human consciousness with its evolved values on the one hand, and the enormous computing power and memory of artificial systems on the other. One cannot help but muse on this subject. It has taken a half billion years for nature to increase the computing power of the brains of animals to their present state. This has been done by the ever-so-slow process of allowing chance DNA mutations to create new forms of life that have greater brain complexity and power than their predecessors. This is what we would call an example of natural animal evolution. Now along come humans with the greatest brain power the Earth has ever seen, and they start to meddle with their brain's own basic building plan. Will these humans do mischief? It looks as though they are about to advance evolution at an alarming rate. Instant changes by genetic engineering rather than natural mutations over the course of millions of years. Computers whose power has been doubling every one and a half years or so will contribute to this sudden jump in the speed of evolution because there is a possibility of connecting computers directly to the brain [25]. It seems reasonable to predict that soon the game of life will be played by different rules. One can imagine Darwin counseling us: "You better learn to adapt fast to the changes you are making, or else you could be preparing the stage for the next act which will be presented with no human actors!"

REFERENCES

1. H. Smith, *The Religions of Man,* Harper Perennial, New York, 1986.
2. A. W. Ham, *Histology,* J. B. Lippincott, Philadelphia, 1965.
3. J. M. Woram, *Sound Recording Handbook,* Howard W. Sams & Co., Indiana, 1989.
4. D. Purves, G. Augustine, and D. Fitzpatrick, *Neuroscience* (2nd Edition), Duke University Medical Center, North Carolina, January 2001.
5. M. E. Raichle, Visualizing the Mind, *Scientific American,* pp. 58-64, April 1994.
6. H. I. Posner and M. E. Raichle, *Images of Mind,* W. H. Feeman, New York, 1994.
7. N. K. Logothitis, Vision: A Window on Consciousness, *Scientific American,* p. 74, November 1999.

8. A. R. Damasio, *The Feeling of What Happens,* Harcourt Brace, New York, 1999.
9. F. Crick and C. Koch, The Problem of Consciousness, *Scientific American,* p. 152, September 1992.
10. J. Wakefield, A Mind for Consciousness, *Scientific American,* p. 37, July 2001.
11. J. Huttlocher, Smart Genes, *Time,* September 13, 1999.
12. M. D. Lemonick, Smart Genes, *Time,* September 13, 1999.
13. M. J. Duff, The Theory Formerly Known as Strings, *Scientific American,* p. 66, February 1998.
14. S. Weinberg, *Dreams of a Final Theory,* Pantheon Books, New York, p. 25, 1992.
15. L. M. Krauss, Cosmological Antigravity, *Scientific American,* p. 55, January 1999.
16. H. Genz, *Nothingness,* Perseus Books, Massachusetts, 1998.
17. D. Chalmers, The Puzzle of Conscious Experience, *Scientific American,* pp. 80-85, December 1995.
18. F. Dyson, *Origins of Life,* Cambridge University Press, New York, 1999.
19. J. Hick, *Death and Eternal Life,* Collins, London, 1976.
20. J. R. Adams, *Surviving Death,* Sterling House, Pittsburgh, Pennsylvania, pp. 101-105, 1998.
21. S. Franklin, *Artificial Minds,* MIT Press, Massachusetts, 1995.
22. D. B. Lenat, Artificial Intelligence, *Scientific American,* pp. 80-82, September 1995.
23. R. Wright, Can Machines Think? *Time,* pp. 50-58, April 1, 1996.
24. R. Kurzweil, The Virtual Thomas Edison, *Time,* December 4, 2000.
25. M. Minsky, Will Robots Inherit the Earth? *Scientific American,* pp. 108-113, October 1994.

CHAPTER 6

What, Where, Why?

This will be a very short chapter, just to comment on what's coming up. It is a sort of road map of where we're going in the chapters that follow.

In the next chapters we are going to hold this Universe up for examination by both microscope and telescope. I am going to ask how you and I fit into the overall structure of particles, energy, and space that surrounds us and exists within us. To help with the investigation, I will be guided by several simple but penetrating questions posed a century and a half ago by the Danish philosopher Soren Kierkegaard. The questions are:

> Where am I? Who am I? How did I come to be here? What is this thing called the world? How did I come into the world? Why was I not consulted? And if I am compelled to take part in it, where is the manager? I would like to see him [1, p. 267].
>
> Soren Kierkegaard 1813-1855

Today these questions remain basic to understanding existence and are to a large extent still unanswered. However, a lot of scientific information has been gathered in the last hundred and fifty years that permits us to look at Kierkegaard's questions in a new light rather than strictly the traditional, religious one.

Kierkegaard's questions are essentially about the "what," "where," and "why" of existence on Earth. It is noteworthy that they don't include the question: what happens to me when I die?

Kierkegaard himself didn't believe that humans had the capacity for finding out anything objective about life after death. As far as he was concerned, the necessary evidence was just not available from which humans could draw objective conclusions about such a subject. According to Kierkegaard, questions as to whether or not existence after death takes place must be decided by each individual on the basis of his or her faith.

Despite Kierkegaard's convictions in this matter, his questions seem well suited to the investigation of our universe. I will use these questions one by one in the three following chapters to try to bring together what we know about life, the universe, and death, and to integrate this knowledge with the ideas and predictions of the Saved Consciousness Hypothesis.

REFERENCE

1. C. Wilson, *Afterlife,* Doubleday, New York, 1987.

CHAPTER 7

How Did I Come Into the World? Who Am I?

This chapter is about you and me, what we are doing here, how we came here, where we're going.

I am standing here today, alive, drinking in everything around me, the wonders and horrors of the world, with my five senses and my brain. They tell me a lot, but they don't tell me what it's all about, where I fit in, how it is that I am here. I know of course that I came from my mother's womb, and she from hers, but how far back does it go, and what does it all mean?

LIFE'S BEGINNINGS

According to Louis Pasteur [cited in 1], all life arises from pre-existing life. He was the first to show this. Every living thing has a parent. Therefore there must be an unbroken chain of connections between me and the first living creatures on Earth. Almost all scientists today agree with Pasteur's findings that life does not arise spontaneously. Life comes from life. It was only recently that people thought bugs, beetles, and so on were created out of the soil without needing parents. Pasteur's work and modern science has put this myth to rest. We need parents.

If this is so, then my roots and your roots go back three and a half billion years or more to the first life on Earth. We have found fossil remains of living things that go back that far [2]. You and I are directly connected to creatures like this through trillions upon trillions of cell divisions over time. The reason I don't look like a single-celled microbe is because of mutations (changes) in the early cells that have allowed them to attach to one another and build larger, more specialized forms of life like us.

This scenario does not agree with any literal translation of the Bible, for the Bible teaches that all kinds of life were created in their present image and have not changed over the years. Bugs were always bugs, horses were horses, humans were humans, and so forth. This is not what most people think today. Our modern belief, as I have said, is that life does not arise spontaneously. Life comes from life. Most scientists agree that there is an unbroken chain of living protoplasm connecting us to the earliest forms of life on Earth. The division of those primitive cells, and the countless mutations in those cells as they continued to divide, are the reason for our existence. That is the long, slow process by which we came into the world and stand here today.

This being so, we seem to have a serious puzzle on our hands. Life comes from life, right? Then how did life start out in the first place? How could it come from life when there was no life? There was not always life on Earth.

It seems, then, that Pasteur's finding that every living thing must have a parent may not apply to the first organisms on Earth unless these organisms came from outside the Earth, from another planet or star system [3, 4]. Although this is possible, it is generally believed that our life originated on Earth, not outside it.

It would be easier to accept this belief if we could show in the laboratory that life can be assembled from inanimate materials. Put some simple chemicals into a pot, turn up the heat, and watch them turn into living things.

A serious attempt to do this was carried out in the middle of the last century by Stanley Miller [cited in 5; see also 6] who heated water and its vapor with methane, ammonia, and hydrogen to mimic early conditions on the planet. He then sent bolts of electricity sparking through this mixture of gases to imitate lightning strikes. No life appeared. Other experiments since then have also failed to produce life, but scientists will keep trying. Some think that the building blocks that form life might have been brought and held together in tiny pockets of porous rock, or on clay surfaces, where they could assemble with the aid of dissolved minerals [7, pp. 75-85]. Workers who study these things would like to produce a molecule that can copy itself such as DNA does in a living cell. Only by copying itself can a molecule reproduce and multiply. This is presumably what happened when life took hold on Earth and eventually transformed into ourselves. So the first replicating molecule may have been the humble beginning of you and me.

Meteorites from outer space that have struck Earth are shown to contain certain molecules essential for life, like hydrocarbons, amino acids, and nucleotides. These meteorites and other bodies from space landed in huge numbers on the early planet adding to the supply of molecules that could be used to build living cells. Conditions for putting together life's building materials may have been available in the warm, watery solutions spread across much of the planet's surface half a billion years after the birth of the solar system. The energy needed to put together these building blocks of life was plentiful. The early Earth was all about raw energy. It was available in large amounts from the hot Sun, violent electrical storms, erupting volcanoes, hydrothermal vents, and space junk raining down from the sky in the form of rocks.

So we had the materials on the Earth's surface to form living cells, and the energy to cement these materials together. Is that what happened three and a half billion years ago in the violent days of Earth's early existence? Were molecules similar to DNA somehow formed in microscopic rock pockets, or in the surface foam of the sea? Was there some catalyst present in this sheltered environment that enabled these molecules to copy themselves? "Fat chance!" said the late Sir Fred Hoyle, Nobel prizewinner, who scoffed that the spontaneous generation of life on Earth would have been as likely as the assemblage of a 747 airliner by a tornado passing through a junkyard. Hoyle argued that microbes exist in space, and that these were the origin of life on Earth. In other words, you and I may have started in space, not on Earth. Before the debate about the beginnings of life is settled, new evidence is needed.

Up to this point, we have looked at possibilities for the beginnings of life as we know it. In case you have forgotten, I am trying in this chapter to address Kierkegaard's questions, "How did I come into the world?" and "Who am I?" I have told you that most modern scientists believe that humans are connected by an unbroken chain of protoplasm to microbes that appeared very early in this planet's history. Assuming this is so, how does a microbe turn itself into a human? It seems like an impossible thing to do, and that is why Darwin's theory of evolution first met with great skepticism. Remember the "monkey trial" early in the last century when an American school teacher was put on trial for teaching that man was related to the monkey? The teacher lost, but the law by which he was convicted was repealed thirty years later [8, 9].

Modern genetics have confirmed that man is related to the monkey and also to all other living things. There is overwhelming evidence. Let's look at the story of this evidence, the story of evolution. It will be a brief glimpse, omitting the details of painstaking research that would fill thousands of volumes.

Once life, in the form of single-celled creatures, got a foothold on this globe, it did very well for itself. It flourished, but it didn't do much in the way of changing its form. It didn't turn into plants and animals for a very long time. It remained in the simple form of free-living, individual cells for three billion years [10, pp. 44-46]. To give a sense of how long this is, a human's average lifespan today is less than eighty years, so three billion years of single cells swarming around the globe would cover many human lifetimes.

At this point in life's history, a stunning change occurred. In a second of time, as it were, life on Earth exploded into a great variety of forms [11-13]. Instead of single cells, a new kind of life had arrived. This life was made up of many cells attached together to form bodies. One could see here, perhaps, the first serious move toward the emergence of you and me.

Now, let's stand back for a moment to look at three very different periods in the history of the Earth.

Period one, lasting about four hundred million years. The surface of the Earth had no life but lots of action in the form of heavenly bodies raining down like nuclear bombs, and erupting volcanoes spreading seas of molten lava right and left. It was possibly an interesting place to visit (in a space ship) but not a friendly place to live.

Period two, lasting about three billion years. The appearance and flourishing of single living cells, monotonous in their uniformity, rather limited in what they could do, but real life nevertheless. At first the DNA of these cells was free-floating in the cytoplasm like the microbes of today. Only in the second half of this three billion year period did the cells develop a nucleus to contain the DNA.

Period three, lasting about six hundred million years (to the present). This was the period when organisms made up of many cells (ferns, trees, worms, fish, dinosaurs, humans) appeared. No longer a barren landscape of rock, water, and microscopic cells, but a rich mix of foliage and animals. The animals set about chasing and eating each other, and also consuming the foliage. What a change to the surface of the world. A kind of complicated, self-adjusting arrangement of dog-eat-dog which we dignify with the name of ecosystem.

Single celled life continued to flourish as before, with a new twist. Some of it took advantage of a fresh opportunity, and lived as parasites upon the multi-celled animals with which they co-existed. An example would be the bacteria in our gut. It has been said that there are more bacteria in the intestine of one human being than the total number of humans that ever lived [12, p. 87]. Although free-living single cells have always been king of the world in numbers, multi-celled life has exploded into the king of diversity.

I use the word "exploded," because that suggests how suddenly these many-celled, multi-shaped creatures arose from the monotonous army of single cells. It is as if small roots in the ground shot forth in a second of time to suddenly become a fully formed tree. This explosive blossoming of diversity happened within a five million year period. That's relatively short. It's small potatoes compared to the three billion years of single celled life preceding it, and the six hundred million year period of slow change that followed it to the present time.

So what do we have? Three billion years of single cell monotony followed by five million (not billion) years of frenzied evolutionary activity. The rest of period three, say five hundred and ninety-five million years, was a time of slow refinement. This refinement included the creation of the human being.

So far in this chapter we have looked briefly at evolution [14-16]. I have said that we humans are connected by a thread of protoplasm to the first creatures on Earth. I have made no attempt to explain how those single celled creatures turned into us. What is the method, the mechanism, that nature has used to achieve this apparent miracle? If this cannot be explained, then evolution is not credible. How do you turn a microbe into a human? If there is a credible explanation, then I think that's a step toward answering Kierkegaard's question: *How did I come into the world?*

In a word, the explanation is: mutation. By this I mean the mutation (which means change) of the long, stringy molecule called DNA. DNA is the blueprint of our body. It is the architect of everything physical that is in us. A change (or mutation) of the DNA in the parent's reproductive cell causes the offspring to be different because the blueprint of its body has changed. Trillions of such changes can mean the difference between a microbe and, say, a dinosaur. That is where Darwin comes in.

DARWIN
(cited in 17, see also 18)

Darwin, of course, is the big name in evolution. He turned the understanding of life on the planet on its ear when he wrote "On The Origin of Species," published in 1857. This book was the story, backed by solid evidence, of how one animal became another. This evidence is believed by most scientists to discredit the idea previously held that all forms of life were created at the same time and did not change after that. Darwin's story pointed to continuous change. It is perhaps one of the most dramatic insights into life that we have.

What did this man do that was so extraordinary? Looking back at it all, it seems like child's play, but he was the first to do the proper research to back up his idea of evolution, changing it from fancy to fact. The idea was this. We observe that parents often pass along their traits, or individual characteristics, to some of their offspring. This could be the color of their eyes, the shape of their claws, their skill at swimming, or whatever. We all know this, so there is no breakthrough there. But Darwin noted that sometimes a new and different trait was seen in a single individual that was not present in the parent or ancestors. This trait was then passed on by that one individual to some of its offspring, and those offspring with the new trait passed it on to their offspring, and soon we have more and more specimens with this trait. What has been created is a new, different trait or characteristic in a group of animals or plants starting from just one individual. This individual has formed a new line of creatures.

So what? Well, let's suppose that the new trait gave that group of animals a survival advantage in the rough and tumble of competitive existence. Let's think of an example. Suppose a certain seal is born with a new trait, say the ability to swim deeper and longer underwater than other seals. That seal will find the hunting good. It will be able to find food when other seals may be starving. It will pass on this deep diving trait to its offspring. Now we will have a lot of lucky, well fed, deep diving seals on the one hand, and starving, shallow diving seals on the other. The deep divers will survive and flourish, the shallow divers will starve and wither. Thus we have the creation of a new species with a new, useful trait, and possibly the extinction of the old that did not have this trait.

The seal example is an imaginative one to show how the idea works. Darwin produced the evidence to show that the idea does actually work and is, in fact, the way new species are created. New traits appear in one individual and, if those traits are adaptive, they permit the lucky individual and its progeny to survive at the expense of those without it. The idea can be grasped by the well known phrase *survival of the fittest.* This phrase is what many of us think of when we think of Darwin. It simply means that those blessed with a new trait that helps them in their struggle to live are the ones that will live and give birth to others with the same new trait that will also survive.

MUTATIONS AND DNA [19-23]

This answers part of the question: how did microbe become man? The answer we have come up with is "mutations." Trillions upon trillions of tiny mutations, the creation of new traits, have produced humans from their single-celled ancestors. Well, the mainstream of science agrees on this. But do we know how these mutations come about? What causes them? What is the reason for a new trait to occur in a single animal when that trait was not present in its parents or ancestors? Do we know?

Yes, we know. It is changes to one or more of the DNA molecules in the parent reproductive cell. Darwin was in the dark about this because he didn't know anything about DNA. It was a molecule whose structure was discovered nearly a hundred years after his time. Darwin didn't have any idea how these new traits suddenly appeared in an individual. He knew that they were passed on after mysteriously appearing in a parent, but how did the parent get them in the first place? Why did they turn up in the parent? He couldn't figure it out, but he called it "heritable variability" just to put a label on it. *Variability* indicated that it was a new trait, and *heritable* showed that the trait was passed on to the following generations. The details of heritable variability gradually became clear, not to Darwin but to his successors.

People working in this field were geneticists and biochemists. There were many, and they slowly put together the pieces of the puzzle of how microbes became man. Heritable variability, observed by Darwin but not understood by him, was found to be caused by factors located in the chromosomes of cells. These factors controlled the body's shape and function. When they changed, the body changed. But why would they change? What causes these mysterious factors in the chromosomes to change in the parent who then passes on the changes to the next generation?

It was known that radiation, whether from natural or man made sources, could cause the hidden factors in the chromosomes of the cell to change (mutate), and this change, if it happened in a parent's reproductive cell, would turn up in the offspring. Much of this information was obtained by exposing fruit flies to radiation, and observing how individuals in the next generation were changed, whether by eye color, wing shape, or other traits. Scientists were now closing in on the puzzle of how new traits are formed. The next question was, by what mechanism did radiation change these factors in the chromosomes? And how do these altered factors change the shape and characteristics of the body?

That is the story of DNA. These mysterious controlling factors in the chromosomes were found to be long, thread like molecules called DNA.

Let's look at DNA more closely. What is it? It is a single molecule made up of many smaller molecules that are put together like a ladder, a very long ladder resembling a fireman's ladder that seems to be endless. Each side of the ladder is made of a long chain of two kinds of molecules, namely, ribose and phosphate. The rungs of the ladder upon which the fireman climbs step by step are made of four kinds of molecules each of which I will abbreviate by a single letter: A, T, G, C. These four molecules are called nucleotides. So what do we have? A long ladder called DNA (the full name for DNA is deoxyribonucleic acid) whose two sides, made of ribose and phosphate, are held together by cross-linking rungs called nucleotides. These nucleotides are A, T, G, and C. That will do for now for the structure of DNA.

We are getting to the point I wish to make, and that point concerns proteins. The DNA ladder contains the instructions for making proteins, all the various kinds that are found in the body. DNA churns out proteins like loaves of bread in a bakery, for that is its principal job.

My body and your body each depends on proteins for its structure. Proteins are the main building blocks of the body. The instructions for building these proteins are found in the rungs of the DNA ladder. If these rungs are changed in any way, then that will alter the instructions given by the DNA for making proteins.

Why would the rungs be changed? What might change them? One common cause is radiation hits. A DNA molecule bombarded by radiation can be damaged where it hurts most: the rungs of the ladder. If this incoming radiation hits the DNA in reproductive cells (ovaries, testes), it may damage the DNA. The damaged DNA could then produce altered proteins in the offspring which might show up as new traits. If the new traits help the offspring survive and adapt to new surroundings, and if further new traits are accumulated from generation to generation, then a new species is eventually created. The formation in this way of new species, and the extinction of old, is the ongoing process of evolution.

Microbe to man is the result of trillions of changes in DNA accumulating over four billion years, mostly during the last six hundred million. These changes to DNA are not only caused by radiation but can be produced in a variety of ways such as duplication errors when DNA divides, or damage to DNA by harmful chemicals in the cells. The precise details of how DNA instructs the synthesis of proteins, how the instructions are passed from one generation to the next, and how proteins function in the body may be found in textbooks of genetics and biochemistry [12]. A brief review is included at the end of this book in Appendix II.

The purpose of this chapter so far has been to provide an overall, bird's eye scan of the role of mutations on evolution, the extraordinary method which Nature has used to create a stunning diversity of animals and plants on Earth. Kierkegaard's question *how did I come into the world* which was posed at the beginning of the chapter has now been answered in part. This question was about *phylogeny* [24, p. 26] which is the word used for the development of all forms of life from the first single cells on Earth to what we see today. Phylogeny is a tree whose roots are the original single-celled creatures and the branches and leaves are the diverse animals and plants that have resulted from those humble, early beginnings.

It is now time to move on to the idea of *ontogeny* [24, p. 107], the word used for the development of a single individual. This is getting personal.

Who am I? asked Kierkegaard. We will start the answer with a brief look at what, rather than who, we are. The "who" will come later, because the "who" is a consequence of "what."

The "what" of someone (sexually bred) begins when a sperm cell from the father enters an egg cell of the mother. A new individual is created containing DNA from both parents, and this makes the new individual different from either parent. At this point the new individual is only a single cell, a cell that is free-living and unattached to any other cell like its ancestors in the seas of early Earth. Then this single cell divides in two, but the two cells don't buzz off, each going its own way. On the contrary, they stay attached to each other, cooperating for their survival. The two become four, the four eight, until a whole body is formed of many trillions of cells.

I will remind you that this did not happen in the early story of life. At that time, cells lived their own separate lives. When DNA mutations finally instructed them to attach to one another, they co-operated in the building of bone, muscle, liver, kidney, brain, and so on, all working together in a coordinated way to produce you or me. That is "what" we are. These cooperating cells are the raw materials, the machinery, the objective parts of a person.

But what about the subjective part, the sense of self that emerges? I believe this subjective feeling is the *who* of Kierkegaard's question, "Who am I?"

THE SUBJECTIVE PART OF ME

The "what" of me is, to some extent, dispensable. I can lose an arm, or a leg, or have someone else's liver or kidney transplanted into me, and the "what" is changed, but not the "who." I have held on to the feeling of "who" I am, my identity, which seems to me to be the same thing as my consciousness. When consciousness is lost, I have lost my identity, the "who" of me. For example, if I faint, I am unconscious. No more "who," no more "me." The object remains, the "what," the materials and machinery of the body, but where is the subjective sense of me, Kierkegaard's "who"? It is lost when we faint, are in a coma, or when we are anesthetized. Where does it go? This may sound like a pointless question, but I ask it simply to focus on the apparent distinction between the functioning body and the functioning sense of self.

Please notice that I used the words "apparent distinction" because there is no known real distinction between body and self. The self is something that *emerges* from the functions of the body and brain. It is connected to the brain. Without the brain, there is no self that we know of in this world.

What are we talking about here? We are talking about Kierkgaard's question, "Who am I"? We assume he was wondering about his subjective sense of self rather than his body or its parts. But this sense of self, this consciousness, is part of the brain, the part that does not work any more when we faint. Which part is it? Science would like to know which part of the brain forms consciousness.

In chapter 5, I presented my own ideas in answer to this question. You may remember that I proposed the existence of a consciousness voltage wave that is the final common pathway of a whole lot of different voltage waves wandering around in the brain. The various voltage waves that were originally triggered by the five senses and the memory networks are processed throughout the brain but, according to my Saved Consciousness Hypothesis, are superposed on a final common pathway, the consciousness wave.

When talking about a consciousness wave, I am referring to something objective and potentially measurable, namely, voltage changes. Billions of voltage changes generated by senses, memory, and processing networks of the brain converging to form a single wave. The movement of electricity, an objective rather than subjective thing. Where, then, does the subjective feeling come from?

What is subjective? As I see it, it involves the emotions of love, hate, anger, grief, and joy. It has to do with reflecting upon our past, present, and future. It is our sense of pain, pleasure, fear, and awe. It is concerned with our ambitions for family, job, security, and happiness. These all appear to emerge from the single, alleged consciousness wave. But how? How does an oscillating voltage produce subjective consciousness? I am confident Kierkegaard would ask that, although he might despair of the human ability to find the answer.

Scientists call this the "hard question." The fact that we don't have an answer doesn't mean that there isn't one. When something is happening and we don't know what, it is often convenient to talk about a black box. It is black because we can't see what is going on inside. We know what we put into the box, and we know what we get out, but what goes on inside is a mystery. In chapter 5, you may recall that I put a black box in the brain. It received the objective consciousness wave as input, and turned it into subjective consciousness. There is no known information to show what might go on inside that box or where in the brain it might be located. If it exists, as I believe it must, it is likely to be spread out in various networks rather than localized in one small region of the brain. I propose that the result of processing the voltages of the final common pathway by this black box is what we feel as subjective consciousness, namely, the awareness of identity or self that every individual with a fully functioning brain possesses. The input to the black box is a single voltage wave. Inside the box, this wave is converted to the subjective feeling of consciousness. This subjective feeling of consciousness, with access to the memories of our past and all the emotions they evoke, perhaps comes close to the "who" of Kierkegaard's question.

Where have we been in this chapter? Here is a brief summary. We started about four billion years ago when single cells were the only living things on Earth. Next, we followed the tree of phylogeny as these single cells formed the multi-celled creatures of today. Then we looked at the tree of ontogeny whereby each individual starts as a single cell and then grows a whole body of many cells. Finally I postulated the existence of a final common voltage pathway in the brain called the objective consciousness wave, proposing that this wave was processed by a subjective black box into what you and I call consciousness. The trip from early Earth to the black box of subjective consciousness has not dealt with details of the landscape on the way, but includes some of the turning points in the evolution of life on this planet. Kierkegaard's question, "Who am I?" has been answered to the degree that science, and some personal speculation on my part, is able to answer it at the present time.

But what about tomorrow? It is unlikely that we have reached the end of this evolutionary process, unlikely that the tree of phylogeny is complete. The DNA of all organisms will continue to mutate, and new species will continue to be created while old ones are removed [25-27]. Scientists will poke and pull at our DNA, and fiddle with artificial intelligence. There is little doubt that life will continue to change, whether by nature's hand or the hand of humans. Who we are today is probably not who we will be tomorrow.

It was mentioned a little while back that without a brain there appears to be no consciousness in this world. We know this from our own experience. We have no recollection of being conscious before we were born, or when we faint. That is a fact, and we can't change facts. Then what about consciousness after death? The brain has stopped functioning, so how can we be conscious?

You may recall my hypothetical answer to this apparent puzzle from chapter 5. It was proposed there that the consciousness voltages inside the brain are continuously transferred from the functioning flesh during life and embedded in a subatomic quantum field, potentially for later replay. It was further postulated that our subjective recall after death may be the result of processing these playback voltages by a black box in subatomic space analogous to the subjective box alleged to be in the brain.

So much for consciousness, its origin and its fate. So much for the "who" of what I am. So much for the existence in a subatomic location for this "who" when the body is dead. But the universe and all its space covers a lot of territory. Where is this subatomic space that may house the consciousness of the dead?

Kierkegaard surely wanted to know something more about the mysteries of the universe when he asked, *Where am I* and *What is this thing called the world?* He was a curious curmudgeon. If he were with us today, he could read in the next chapter many newly discovered things about the universe that would surely surprise and possibly intrigue him. If he were aware of today's knowledge about the universe, he might think that we may yet discover the home of the dead.

REFERENCES

1. H. Cuny, *Louis Pasteur: The Man and His Theories,* Eriksson, New York, 1966.
2. J. Horgan, Off to an Early Start, *Scientific American,* p. 24, August 1993.
3. M. Alpert, Heavenly Seeds, *Scientific American,* p. 29, April 2001.
4. J. Horgan, The Return of the Maverick, *Scientific American,* pp. 46-47, March 1995.
5. J. Rebek, Jr., Synthetic Self-Replicating Molecules, *Scientific American,* pp. 48-55, July 1994.
6. L. E. Orgel, The Origin of Life on Earth, *Scientific American,* pp. 78-79, October 1994.
7. R. M. Hazen, Life's Rocky Start, *Scientific American,* pp. 75-85, April 2001.
8. K. Tierney, *Darrow: A Biography,* Crowell, New York, 1979.
9. N. M. Blake, Bryan, *The World Book Encyclopedia* (Vol. 2), Chicago, p. 543, 1983.
10. M. Nash, How Did Life Begin? *Time,* pp. 44-46, October 11, 1993.
11. J. S. Levinton, The Big Bang of Animal Evolution, *Scientific American,* pp. 84-91, November 1992.

12. S. J. Gould, The Evolution of Life on the Earth, *Scientific American*, pp. 84-91, October 1994.
13. M. Nash, When Life Exploded, *Time*, pp. 38-46, December 4, 1995.
14. W. Howells, *Getting Here: The Story of Human Evolution*, Compass Press, Washington, D.C., 1997.
15. I. Tattersall, Once We Were Not Alone, *Scientific American*, pp. 56-62, January 2000.
16. M. Lemonik and A. Dorfman, Up from the Apes, *Time*, pp. 30-38, August 23, 1999.
17. C. M. Pond, Darwin, Charles Robert, *The World Book Encyclopedia* (Vol. 5), Chicago, pp. 32-33, 1983.
18. G. De Beer, *Charles Darwin: Evolution by Natural Selection*, Greenwood, Connecticut, 1976.
19. J. D. Watson, *The Double Helix*, Atheneum, New York, 1968.
20. E. Frankel, *DNA: The Ladder of Life*, McGraw, New York, 1979.
21. D. L. Hartl, Heredity, *The World Book Encyclopedia* (Vol. 9), Chicago, pp. 192f-196, 1983.
22. E. Rubenstein, Cell, *The World Book Encyclopedia* (Vol. 3), Chicago, pp. 250g-250l, 1983.
23. M. Lemonick and D. Thompson, Racing to Map our DNA, *Time*, pp. 28-34, January 1999.
24. L. A. Adams and S. Eddy, *Comparative Anatomy*, John Wiley & Sons, New York, 1949.
25. D. H. Erwin, The Mother of Mass Extinctions, *Scientific American*, pp. 72-78, July 1996.
26. E. O. Wilson, Vanishing Before Our Eyes, *Time* Special Edition, pp. 29-31, April-May 2000.
27. R. M. May, How Many Species Inhabit the Earth, *Scientific American*, pp. 42-48, October 1992.

CHAPTER 8

Where Am I? What is This Thing Called the World?

Where am I? The question is good, but the answer not obvious. Even though standing on solid ground, I am weaving a zig-zag course through the Universe. Forget the solid ground. Put me on a merry-go-round instead, and put the merry-go-round on a cruise ship. Hey, look at me move! But the cruise ship moves with the world as the planet turns on its axis. Wow, look at me move now! Still we're not finished. The Earth orbits the sun, the sun revolves with the galaxy, the galaxy careens through space as it flies away from other galaxies. . . . Look, Ma, no hands! So where am I? Kierkegaard didn't know, and he wanted to know. Today, we know more than he did, but are still just nibbling at the edges. Future scientists will not be bored as they continue to nibble.

Where do we think we are? The ancients figured it out with their eyes, no help from telescopes. They were on a flat world, they thought, covered by a ceiling sprinkled with lights. Well, as you know, they were wrong. The world is round, and there is no ceiling. So, granted the world is round, then the sun and the lights in the sky are turning around the world, right? Wrong again, as you know. The world is turning around the sun, and the lights (stars) appear to be moving because the world is spinning like a top. It's not those lights in the sky that are turning, it's us.

Please accompany me and my notepad as we take a short inventory of the universe in the light of today's knowledge. We will look at where we are located using our intuition (unreliable), the evidence we have gathered (reliable), and our interpretation of the evidence (partly reliable).

This inventory will be a brief and, of course, an incomplete one, intended only to try to give the big picture. Professional astronomers have devoted careers to the study of things that I hardly mention, such as binary stars, stellar winds, neutrinos, vacuum energy, novae, supernovae, accretion disks, pulsars, event horizons, and mini-black holes. So, recognizing that the devil is in the details, I will nevertheless steer clear of details so that we can cover a reasonable amount of ground, and cover it fast. Finally, not being an astronomer, my own knowledge is strictly limited and I am prepared to take a lot of flak from you. This being said, let's proceed and shoot for the big picture starting with what was derisively called by astrophysicist Fred Hoyle the "big bang."

THE BIG BANG

Our common sense tells us that the universe had to start somewhere, somehow. The stars and other heavenly things like the Earth, asteroids, comets, and the energy that moves them around must have had a beginning. Our intuition would like us to believe that the universe, similar to other things, had a start. Well, science has come up with a theory, the theory of the Big Bang [1, pp. 62-70; 2] that seems to confirm our intuition. This theory is more or less accepted as fact by most scientists today. It is based on the idea that everything in the universe *(everything!)* was once gathered into a small spot tinier than the period at the end of this sentence. The whole universe. Ridiculous! It goes completely against our common sense, just as a round world seemed ridiculous before Columbus. How could you squeeze all the stars in the sky onto the point of a pin? Well, theory says that you can. When everything in the universe was crammed into that small space, an explosion of unbelievable force took place, sending the whole works outwards in space. The space, which did not exist before the explosion, was created at the same time as the explosion and expanded to receive it. Absurd, say you? Well, that's the theory accepted by many respected scientists today.

There was no actual matter or substance at the time of the Big Bang, only energy in the form of an ionized plasma. Our intuition can perhaps accept the exploding part of the theory. After all, we have seen dynamite at work. The part about cramming the whole universe onto the point of a pin is harder to handle. Should we believe it?

What is the evidence for the Big Bang?

First of all, it was noted by Hubble about eighty years ago that galaxies in the sky (groups of billions of stars) are moving away from each other [3, pp. 162-164], which is just the sort of thing one would expect in an explosion. It has been more recently found that the temperature of space today is what would be expected if there were a Big Bang that had happened about fifteen billion years ago [1, pp. 68-70]. Things cool down at a predictable rate. By noting today's temperature, you can figure out more or less what the temperature was at the moment of the Bib Bang. Hot, very hot, so hot that only energy, not matter, could exist. And the pressure, of course, was great beyond understanding. That's why it has been named the "Mother of all Explosions."

The temperature and pressure at the time of the Big Bang was too great even for atoms to exist. Atoms were made hundreds of thousands of years later, when things had cooled off a bit and electrons and protons could settle down and mate. The simplest atoms, hydrogen and helium atoms, were formed in that cooling "plasma" and thus we had the first appearance of matter. These atoms were not smoothly spread out in space, for some were closer together than others. We have evidence of this clumping from the uneven left-over radiation in space, the smoking gun of the Big Bang called cosmic background radiation [4, 5].

What happened to these early hydrogen and helium atoms scattered in space? Gravity went to work on them, pulling them together in the form of round balls of gas the size of stars. The molecules of gas continued to pack together in each ball creating such enormous heat and pressure that hydrogen atoms eventually fused together to form more helium atoms in a colossal nuclear fireball. The equivalent of trillions of hydrogen bombs. In other words, an ordinary star was born [6-8].

In fact, trillions of stars, not of equal size like jellybeans in a bag, but in a variety of sizes, were born. Some were smaller than the Sun, others hundreds of times bigger. These stars were clustered together in groups called galaxies, which were spread all over the heavens [9-11]. Some of these stars were in the process of being born while others were dying.

Mr. Kierkegaard asks, "Where am I?" Well, it can be said that he was on a planet belonging to one of those stars (the middle-aged Sun), in one of those galaxies (the Milky Way). He was obviously part, as you and I are, of a seething turmoil of matter and energy in this universe.

A natural question: where are all those galaxies of stars headed? Assuming they originated at a single point and are exploding outward, they must be going somewhere. Where will they end up? Does space go on forever? [12].

A limitless universe is hard to imagine. Our intuition tells us it can't go on forever. How can something go on forever? There must be an end to how far the stars, or you, or anything can go without coming to some kind of barrier, edge, or limit. That's what the ancients thought about the world when they believed it was flat. If they went far enough, they would fall off the edge! Columbus proved them wrong. The world is round and there is no edge. In a sense, Albert Einstein was the Columbus of space. His General Theory of Relativity indicates that space is curved [13, chapter 2; 14-16]. The stars in curved space are separating from each other as though they were dots on the curved surface of a balloon. The more you blow up the balloon, the farther apart the dots get. In this sense, there seems to be no barrier or edge to stop those moving dots on the surface of the balloon, or the moving stars in curved space, from separating indefinitely. There seems to be no limit to how far apart those dots or stars can get away from each other. Unless, of course, you stop blowing up the balloon. The degree to which you can blow up that balloon would seem to limit the expansion of the universe.

The balloon does indeed appear to be getting larger as the Big Bang continues to blow it up. We know this because we observe that the galaxies are moving away from us, the farthest ones the fastest. The question that has puzzled astronomers since this outward movement has been known is: will gravity eventually pull all these galaxies together again which would end the Big Bang with a Big Crunch? Will everything return back to a point of unimaginable pressure and temperature where evidence tells us that the universe started? Is our universe in an unending cycle of explosive expansions and then contractions?

There are some astrophysicists that think so [17]. They suggest that our universe is destined to contract again. Furthermore, they would like you to believe that ours is not the only universe around. It is but one of many universes. In their picture, they imagine many universes all interconnected like a lot of bubbles filling space in every direction. The number of these soap-like bubble universes would be like an unending sea of balloons all joined together by narrow necks so that the interior of each balloon would join with the interior of its neighbor, permitting an imaginary traveler to move from bubble to bubble, or universe to universe. If we were to stand back and look at these soap-bubble universes from the outside to see what was going on, we would see a very active group of bubbles all in different stages of contraction and expansion. Each one is born with a Big Bang, exploding outward with incredible energy until the expansion runs its course and it collapses by gravity in a Big Crunch to its original size. The universes, ours being one, all exist at different stages and sizes of this unending cycle of expansions and contractions. The "laws of nature" within each bubble could be quite different from one bubble to the next.

Gravity, temperature, pressure, the speed of light, electromagnetism, and so on could operate quite differently than they do here at home in our universe.

Going back to our intuition, we can imagine such a system of bubble universes without much trouble if the system ended somewhere. If each of the universes starts with a Big Bang, one can visualize it pulling itself together again in a big crunch. The human race has not yet developed instruments or ideas to test such a hypothesis. And it goes against intuition to think that these interconnecting bubbles could extend without end in both space and time. It seems natural to ask, "Are all these bubble universes contained by another, bigger bubble? And what's beyond that? And when do they end in time, and what's beyond that? Are we looking at a perpetual motion machine, a pendulum that cycles back and forth forever, extending without limit, driven by energy interchanging with mass according to Einstein's famous equation $e = mc^2$?"

Who knows? New discoveries keep popping up to upset theories based on previous discoveries. For example, we have recently found a strong argument against a Big Crunch, at least in our universe. It seems that our universe is expanding faster and faster. That is to say, the *rate* of expansion of our universe is increasing. Hubble found out about eighty years ago that the farthest stars were moving outwards faster than the nearer stars, but it now seems that their outward speed, instead of being gradually slowed down by the backward pull of gravity, is actually increasing, as though there were a force counter-acting gravity and pushing them away [18-21]. We are talking about a repulsive force here, stronger than gravity. This repulsive force was worked out by Einstein who called it a "cosmological constant" and later, in an about face, referred to it as his "greatest blunder." In the light of our recent discoveries, it may not have been a blunder at all. The expansion of the universe seems to be accelerating under the influence of this repulsive force.

Recent evidence for the accelerating expansion of our universe comes from the study of very bright exploding stars called supernovae. The way they are spaced throughout the universe suggests that galaxies are receding from each other at ever increasing speeds, the farthest having reached velocities near the speed of light. If they reach the speed of light, they should achieve infinite mass. This is counter-intuitive. On the other hand, we have a conflict of intuition because our intuition says the idea of an accelerating expansion is okay, since the farther the galaxies get separated from each other, the weaker is the force of gravity holding them together. If there were a repulsive force stronger than the enfeebled force of gravity, then galaxies would keep moving faster and faster away from one another. The whole business seems to confuse everybody and has got the cosmology community scrambling for theories.

Another argument can be put up against a future contraction of the universe. It is that we cannot find enough mass in the universe to draw it back together again by gravity in a Big Crunch. This would be true even if there were no repulsive force working against gravity. In order for a Big Crunch to happen, it is calculated that there would have to be more matter in the universe than we can detect. We have had to propose the existence of what we call "dark matter," an imaginary material that does not shine but which has the necessary gravity to cause a Big Crunch [22]. We don't know if such stuff exists or not. From what is known at present about the amount of matter in the universe, it looks as though the universe may go on expanding forever.

As the nuclear fires in stars use up all their fuel and burn out, there will be nothing left in space except black, massive objects hurtling away from each other. This is a bleak interpretation of the evidence but, as we have seen, our ideas continually change as new discoveries alter our interpretation of old findings. Scientists have their work cut out for them in the future to answer Kierkegaard's question, "Where am I?" just as philosophers have their problem looking for a home for the dead.

In our own lives, we are always speculating about the future. We have to, because we have to plan for the future. To prevent catastrophic events from overwhelming us, we must know what catastrophes could come. We ask ourselves, "How do I survive if this happens, or that? I must make preparations. I must figure out in advance what will happen." Partly from habit, partly from a natural sense of curiosity, we carry over this speculation to the future of the universe. It doesn't matter for us personally what the state of the universe will be in a few billion years down the road, but it gives us satisfaction to try and figure it out anyway.

There is too little known about the limits of our universe to make any predictions about its expansion in space. We can only guess at this. However, we are on firmer ground when it comes to understanding the birth and death of objects that are still in the part of the universe that we can observe with our telescopes and other instruments. We can reasonably ask, "What happens to stars as they age? What is going to happen to the Sun and the Earth in the future? What will happen to us, the humans who find themselves adrift in the cosmos, this playground of extraordinary objects and events?" Let's continue with our inventory.

STARS

The Sun is an average star. Its glow keeps us alive, so it plays a very important part in our lives. We would like to know what to expect from the Sun. When will it cease to shine? What is the life history of stars?

Twinkle, twinkle little star. You appear in the heavens wherever I look. The nearest pinpoints of light are single stars. The ones that we can see farther out give more light than a single star, and are mostly groups of stars called galaxies that are found in space out to the edge of the visible universe. It is possible to see these far off galaxies at such great distances because each galaxy contains up to a hundred billion or more stars and therefore gives off a tremendous amount of light. Even so, most galaxies are so far away that powerful telescopes are needed to detect them. If you are looking at the sky with your naked eyes, the billions of galaxies filling the heavens will not be visible to you. You need instruments that are more powerful than your eye in order to see them. With the naked eye, only a tiny fraction of all stars is visible.

Let's ask a few questions about stars. What are they made of? How did those pin-points of light get out there, and what are they doing? What did people think about stars before telescopes and other instruments came along to help us understand them? They really didn't know what to think. Now we think we know.

The interior of the Sun (our star) is very, very hot [23]. I don't have to tell you that. But did you know that the center of the Sun is about fifteen million degrees Celsius? May we take a look to see how it got that way? This is how.

The Sun formed out of hydrogen gas left over from the Big Bang. All stars formed that way. The hydrogen gas separated into huge balls, each of which was squeezed so tightly by its own gravity that it became very hot, hot enough to ignite its hydrogen by thermonuclear fusion. Thermonuclear fusion means that the hot hydrogen atoms, stripped of their electrons by the heat, rammed into one another with such fury that they fused together. The result of this fusion of hydrogen atoms was to form helium atoms (slightly bigger) and to release a colossal amount of heat. Like umpteen zillion hydrogen bombs going off in regular sequence without stop. With all this heat, is there any wonder that the Sun can warm up the Earth nearly a hundred million miles away?

This ongoing process of thermonuclear fusion in the Sun has continued steadily for about five billion years to the present day, and will probably continue for five billion more before the Sun has converted all its hydrogen to helium and run out of fuel.

Thermonuclear fusion is what makes the Sun shine, and makes other stars shine also. That is why we stand here on Earth on a dark, cloudless night and see a sky filled with needle-points of light, the twinkling light of burning stars. People living near one of those distant stars would see our Sun as a needle-point of light in their sky. The Earth would not be visible to them because it is not on fire and only reflects a few of the Sun's rays, far too feeble a light to see from the distance of an observer near another star.

RED GIANTS

What will happen when the Sun has burned up all, or most, of its hydrogen? Normally, we would expect the nuclear fires on the Sun to go out in such a case, and the planets orbiting the Sun to go into a deep-freeze. Will this happen? No, this is not what will happen. On the contrary, the planets, at least the nearer ones, will probably burn to a crisp. The Sun will turn into what is called a Red Giant [24], swallowing up and vaporizing the planets that are nearest to it, including the Earth. Here is why.

Let's say you are warming yourself by the fire on a cold day. When the wood is all burned, the fire goes out, if you let it. But you don't. You put some more wood in, and the fire heats up again. We can compare this to what will happen in the Sun when it forms a Red Giant. There are several things to know.

First. It is only in the center of the Sun that hydrogen burns to form helium. This goes on slowly but steadily over billions of years and forms the heat that warms us on Earth. The heat also forms a pressure pushing outwards from the center that prevents the Sun from collapsing by its own gravity. We call this "thermonuclear pressure" because it is formed by the tremendous heat released by the fusion of hydrogen nuclei. It's what holds the sun up like air in a balloon.

Second. When the hydrogen is used up in the center of the Sun and the nuclear fires dwindle, the temperature at the center drops, the pressure pushing outwards is reduced, and the Sun therefore contracts, just as though you let air out of the balloon. But this, you may object, is not what should happen if the Sun is to become a Red Giant. It should be getting bigger, not smaller. Okay, let me explain further.

Third. The core is now mostly helium. The hydrogen has fused to form helium. And here is the point to be made: As the Sun contracts at the center because of the dwindling fire, this compaction heats the helium to very high temperatures. The helium, which has replaced the hydrogen, can now start burning. Why didn't it burn before? Because helium needs higher temperatures than hydrogen to burn. Helium burns hotter than hydrogen. This higher temperature is provided by the further contraction of the Sun. Now where are we? We're on the way to becoming a Red Giant, and this is why.

Fourth. The Sun is burning hotter than it was originally, because helium, which has now been ignited, burns hotter than hydrogen. It is as if you had put another log on the fire, only this time you used maple, which burns hotter than spruce. The heat from the helium reaches the outer gaseous envelope of the Sun, making it expand. As it expands, it cools. As it cools, it turns red. Aha! A Red Giant.

That is the story, in simplified form, of how the Sun will turn into a Red Giant. The expanding red envelope of the Sun will reach out and engulf the closest planets and fry them. Although the envelope is much cooler than the Sun's interior, it is hot enough to vaporize the Earth. Don't worry, we won't be here then. This will happen about five billion years down the road.

The Sun is not the only star whose fate will undergo these changes. Of the ten thousand trillion trillion or so stars out there, about ninety percent of them will become Red Giants as they burn up their fuel. What then? What is the fate of a Red Giant? We can find out if we look at what lies in store for the Sun.

WHITE DWARFS

Have you ever thought of the sky as a graveyard? In a sense, that's what it is. The corpses are the burnt out stars, the remaining bodies of dead stars that have exhausted all their fuel. They started out, you will remember, as burning balls of hydrogen gas slowly changing to helium gas by thermonuclear fusion. When the hydrogen is gone, then the helium burns and it, in turn, fuses to form carbon and oxygen. By this time, the star has transformed into a Red Giant and will soon cool and contract to become one of the corpses, or dead stars, that litter the universe. These corpses, that were once bright, shining stars, are now dim and small. They are called white dwarfs [13, chapter 4; 25]. This is what the Sun will become in about five billion years. The Sun, when it becomes a Red Giant, will expand and vaporize the Earth, but will then contract to the size of a White Dwarf. Because its nuclear fires are out, there will be no more hot gas to prevent gravity from squeezing it down to less than a thousandth of its original size. That is what will happen to the Sun five billion years or so from now. It will become one of the White Dwarfs presently littering the universe.

It is not an exaggeration to call the space around us a sort of graveyard, because that is what it is. It is full of cadavers. There are probably as many dead, extinguished stars populating the heavens in every direction as there are living, burning ones. The increasing numbers of cooling, dead stars exist side by side with the living, burning ones.

Now, the subject of "quantum pressure" comes up. This is important when looking at the life history of stars. It would seem natural to ask why gravity does not squeeze the White Dwarf down some more. What stops it? If the nuclear fires are out and can no longer hold up the White Dwarf against the inward squeeze of its own gravity, why doesn't the White Dwarf collapse to an even smaller size?

For those who are interested, the explanation involves something called quantum pressure that in turn involves what is known as Pauli's exclusion principle (Wolfgang Pauli was one of the physicists involved in the early development of quantum mechanics). This is how it goes. After helium is burned out in the core of the Sun to form a White Dwarf, the core of the White Dwarf is then composed of a mixture of carbon and oxygen held up by "quantum pressure." The mixture of carbon and oxygen at the core, which is not burning, cannot be compressed further because no two electrons can occupy the same space, which is Pauli's exclusion principle. The electrons that are being squeezed together cannot be squeezed into the same place. The White Dwarf has gotten as small as it can get, unless it becomes what is called a neutron star.

This is starting to become complicated, isn't it? From ordinary star to Red Giant, to White Dwarf, and now to Neutron Star [13, 26-28].

This occasionally happens. Let me give the reason. If a dead star has a great enough mass, more massive, say, than our Sun, then even quantum pressure and Pauli's exclusion principle will not be strong enough to hold it up when it is squeezed down to the size of a White Dwarf. It will continue to go down in size because the quantum pressure will not be able to resist the tremendous force of gravity. The electrons will be squeezed so hard that they will be absorbed by the proton nuclei to form neutrons. The dead star will collapse to a diameter of thirty miles or so, a tiny fraction of the size of a White Dwarf. Something that started out bigger than the Sun is now only thirty miles across? Hard to imagine.

NEUTRON STARS

This must be getting confusing to the reader, so please let me explain more carefully. What happens when a neutron star forms is this.

The mass of the original Red Giant is so great that, when the nuclear fires go out and the immense force of gravity squeezes it down, the negatively charged electrons in the atoms are pushed into the atom's nucleus, turning the positively charged protons contained by the nucleus into neutrons. The overwhelming pressure of gravity, in other words, has no longer made it possible for the electrons to remain free. The electrons have combined with the protons to make neutrons. A proton with a positive electric charge has fused with an electron with a negative charge, forming a particle with no charge. That is why it is called a neutron. What is now holding this dead star up is neutron pressure, not the electron pressure that holds up a White Dwarf. Wall to wall neutrons is all that's left of what was once a massive, burning star. This left over neutron star is, as I have said, only about thirty miles in diameter, squeezed down from a star, say, a million miles in diameter. Some squeezing! That's what gravity will do if you give it enough mass to work with.

It is interesting that neutron stars, these small, round, massive star remnants, are usually seen to spin at an incredible rate. They can turn, like a spinning top, up to a thousand times per *second* on their own axis. In fact, that's how they were discovered. Some of them, called pulsars, emit a flash of light upon each revolution probably due to what can be called a magnetic field effect. These flashes of light can be seen in the sky, identifying the neutron star and indicating how fast it's spinning. Perhaps we can compare the accelerated spin of the shrinking neutron star with the intensified spin of a skater who draws in her arms and spins faster.

BLACK HOLES [26-28]

Can a neutron star contract any more and get smaller still? Can its thirty-mile diameter get even smaller? Yes, if the neutron star turns into that mysterious, hungry monster we call a Black Hole. Sometimes the colossal pull of gravity continues to collapse the neutron star even further so that it ends up as a Black Hole. Virtually nothing left. The neutron star has vanished but, strangely enough, the gravity that pulled it down to virtually nothing is still there continuing to pull and drag in anything it can get its hands on. The gravity is still there inside the Black Hole. Other than the irresistible pull, the hole is empty with all matter apparently crushed out of existence.

What is going on here anyway? Humans are intrigued and fascinated by great power and great mystery. A Black Hole has both. It certainly has great power since it's capable of swallowing millions, perhaps billions, of stars like our Sun and making them disappear. The great mystery is, where did all those stars go?

We don't have any *direct* evidence that Black Holes exist, for who can see a hole, especially if it's black? However, even if we can't see it, we can see its effects. When someone falls into a hole, we may not see the hole itself but we see the person disappearing. In the case of a Black Hole, we suspect it is there because it affects nearby objects. For example, it swallows the objects, or causes them to emit radiation as they fall inwards, or changes their speed and direction of movement. We see how the hole affects its surroundings. In addressing Kierkegaard's question, "Where am I?," I think Black Holes deserve the attention we are giving them here. They seem to be such an extraordinary part of our universe.

Where are Black Holes found? What do they do? Where are they going? Answers to these questions, however superficial the answers may be, I think will emphasize what an awesome space we live in.

Black Holes arise, as mentioned, from very big, collapsing stars. A massive star, say thirty to a hundred times more massive than our Sun, can completely collapse when it burns out, having exhausted its nuclear fuel at the end of its life. The collapse of the massive star does not halt at the stage of a White Dwarf, or even of a neutron star, because the gravity is so great that the collapsing star pulls itself inwards to the size of nothing, just a Black Hole, with no visible evidence of what was there before.

Einstein's General Theory of Relativity predicts that the matter that formerly made up the massive star compacts into a region of zero volume and infinite density. The hole appears black, because no light escapes from its interior. It is called a hole, because it's empty. It is believed that space and time cease to exist at the center of the hole.

Where are Black Holes found? There is evidence that they exist in our own galaxy, the Milky Way, as well as in other galaxies. There are estimates of up to one hundred black holes in our galaxy that have been formed from the collapse of massive stars. But there are probably a lot more than that because the collapse of single massive stars is not the only source of Black Holes. They can also come from what are called black hole binary systems that are formed when one star, revolving around another, transfers mass to the companion star that eventually collapses under the increasing load to form a Black Hole. It is estimated that there may be up to one thousand of these binary black hole systems in the Milky Way.

The most massive Black Hole in our galaxy appears to occupy the center of the Milky Way where the gravity is found to be far greater than the number of visible stars that could cause this gravity. This indicates that a monster Black Hole has sucked millions, perhaps billions, of stars into its maw and destroyed them. That's what a Black Hole is good at. Each star it swallows makes its gravity stronger so it can reach out farther to grab the next star. Pretty soon all the stars in the neighborhood are vacuumed up. We believe this is going on in the center of our galaxy. We could not live there.

What about the other galaxies of stars in the universe? After all, our galaxy (the Milky Way) is only one of a hundred billion or more detectable galaxies populating the universe. Is the Milky Way the only galaxy in the universe that plays host to these ravenous monsters aptly called Black Holes?

Absolutely not. It is believed that most galaxies have a large Black Hole at their center and many smaller ones spread throughout. If you estimate the number of Black Holes for each galaxy, and multiply that by the number of galaxies in the universe, you end up with a count of hundreds of billions of Black Holes. They are a common and hungry form of beast that is on the loose in our universe eating up stars.

Astronomers think they can detect some Black Holes by X-rays that are formed when space material is dragged toward the hole. This approaching matter encounters strong magnetic fields as it nears the mouth of the hole, emitting X-rays that can be detected as far away as Earth. A particularly good example of this Black Hole radiation is called a quasar [29]. A quasar is the radiation seen around a very massive Black Hole, and it is so bright it can outshine the brightness of a whole galaxy.

Do Black Holes ever pack up and go home? When a Black Hole is formed, does it stay around forever? Apparently, or almost. What goes into the hole doesn't come out. However, Black Holes may radiate away some of their energy by the formation of particle-antiparticle pairs at its mouth ("event horizon"), one of the pair being able to escape the gravity of the hole [30]. But the time it takes to radiate away all the energy of the Black Hole in this way would be longer than the present age of the universe. So don't hold your breath waiting for Black Holes to disappear from the universe.

The singularity, or center, of a Black Hole is thought to have a lot in common with the origin of the universe. According to the theory of the Big Bang, the universe and everything in it started from a singularity. This fits nicely with the ideas of those who are pushing for a "bubble" universe where an infinite number of universes, or bubbles, extend forever in every direction surrounding our own universe. The idea goes like this. The singularity, or center, of a Black Hole explodes in a big bang to form a new universe (such as ours) containing new Black Holes. The Black Holes in the new universe explode, each forming another additional universe with its own Black Holes. With all of these Black Holes exploding and forming their own universes, the result should be an unlimited number of universes each formed from a Black Hole. As mentioned, our universe may be one of them.

Even Darwin gets into the act here with his law of "the survival of the fittest." Those universes with unworkable rules of physics fall by the wayside. Only the fittest universes survive with alternate cycles of bang and bust. Our particular universe, then, may have started from a Black Hole with laws of physics that enabled it to survive, and Black Holes now existing in our universe may give rise to new universes.

There is still a lot going on to try and clarify the physics of Black Holes. The subject is far from settled. Einstein's Theory of General Relativity implies, for example, that the matter entering a Black Hole compacts into a region of zero volume and infinite density at the center. In other words, crammed into a point that has no volume. Nonsense, say some. Such an idea conflicts with quantum theory that says such a point cannot exit because of Heisenberg's Uncertainty Principle. Furthermore, equations containing infinities such as Einstein's equations are suspected of having something wrong with them. The idea of the center of a Black Hole having zero volume and infinite density has consequently been revised. The volume, no matter how small, needs to have some value, perhaps a size smaller than the nucleus of an atom that, although small, is not zero. Similarly, the density must be something less than infinity. This can also be said about the volume and density of the singularity from which our universe was born. The volume, no matter how small, had some value, and the density, regardless of how great, was not infinite.

I would ask you to stand back now. Go out on a dark, serene night and gaze up at the sky. How placid it appears, how tranquil, how reassuring that there is some stability in the world and we don't, after all, live in an environment of upheaval and violence. Is this true? No. How wrong, how wrong! We are deceived to think there is peace and quiet out there. Instead, the sky is a battleground of clashing objects and energy, an angry fight between irresistible forces meeting almost immoveable objects. Stars are being continually born, then crunched out of existence, blown up, or swallowed in Black Holes that vacuum up the centers of galaxies. Pulsars thirty miles in diameter spinning at a rate of one thousand times a second without flying apart because their gravity is too strong to let anything go. Intense radiation bursts from who knows where caused by who knows what. Temperatures of extraordinary extremes, both cold and hot. Collisions of galaxies (we are due to collide with Andromeda in about three billion years). An expansion of the outer limits of the universe apparently accelerating at close to the speed of light. This is all going on around us.

Look up at the sky, again, and ask Kierkegaard's question, "Where am I?" The answer, in part, is: not in a quiet place. It is a place about which we know much more today than Kierkegaard did in his time. If we remain curious and keep up this pace of discovery, we will soon be able to answer Kierkegaard's question about where he is (or was) with increasing accuracy. We set out in this chapter to do this, at least in part.

Is Kierkegaard still around somewhere, even though he died a century and a half ago? Is his mind alive? If so, where? Quantum theory tells us that information can't be lost, not even the information in Kierkegaard's brain. The Saved Consciousness Hypothesis, which is the *raison d'etre* of this book, suggests to us that one's consciousness wave continues to exist, embedded in a quantum field, even after death. Where, in this turbulent environment, could it be? Kierkegaard and Aunt Dorothy's consciousness are presumed to be in subatomic space somewhere in the cosmos that I have described. These departed individuals are not telling us where.

Has Aunt Dorothy met Kierkegaard somewhere in subatomic space? This is of course a futile question because we don't know if either person still exists. We only have grounds to speculate that the consciousness of their past life is still present in the alleged eleven dimensions of subatomic space. But at what location in all space? In what region or regions of this boiling Universe might the subatomic space containing Aunt Dorothy's consciousness be located?

One can propose two possible scenarios. The first scenario says that, as Aunt Dorothy's consciousness wave is being embedded in the subatomic space in her brain during life, this particular region of space travels with her wherever the brain goes. That is to say, the region of subatomic space that holds the consciousness wave stays with the brain. When Aunt Dorothy's brain finally dies, the subatomic space containing her life-long consciousness remains at the spot where the brain expired. Thus, Aunt Dorothy's consciousness wave would, according to this scenario, be expected to reside after death at one fixed location in the universe.

The second scenario I like better. It proposes that, as the brain travels through space, it leaves the consciousness wave trailing behind it as described in chapter 5. The brain may be compared to a boat traveling through water that leaves a wake wherever it goes. We noted at the beginning of this chapter that the brain travels to many places, accompanying the Earth, Sun, and Milky Way in their extensive travels. So, according to scenario number two, the consciousness voltages of a living or departed person, whether Aunt Dorothy or Kierkegaard, would be smeared across the sky in association with the other energy fields that exist there. That's okay. There's no shortage of subatomic space in the sky. The brain, like a boat moving through water, might leave in its wake a permanent voltage record of each moment of consciousness that the brain once held, available for replay after death.

If space itself in this universe should get destroyed as it might in a Big Crunch, what would happen to our embedded consciousness? Might it also be destroyed? This thought was raised in chapter 2. There, the possibility was mentioned that this universe could be connected by "wormholes" to other universes, and that perhaps the voltage patterns of consciousness could escape through them. This thought may be of some comfort to those of us who are reluctant to be separated from our past life.

In our search for life after death, we will now turn to the subject of religion. You have been reading about the Saved Consciousness Hypothesis which, of course, is a new kid on the block. As you know, other schools of thought proposing life after death, particularly those of religion, are thousands of years older and have gained the respect of most of the world. For that reason, it would be the height of arrogance on my part to exclude the teachings of religion in any discussion of life after death. In the next chapter, we'll see a little of what the five major religions have to say about this subject.

REFERENCES

1. S. G. Brush, How Cosmology Became a Science, *Scientific American,* August 1992.
2. J. E. Peebles, D. Schramm, E. Turner, and R. Kron, The Evolution of the Universe, *Scientific American,* Special Issue, pp. 52-57, October 1994.
3. A. D. Aczel, *God's Equation,* Four Walls Eight Windows, New York, 1999.
4. C. S. Powell, The Golden Age of Cosmology, *Scientific American,* pp. 17-22, July 1992.
5. N. Mandolisi and N. Vittorio *The Cosmic Microwave Background,* Kluwer Academic Publishers, New York, 1990.
6. T. P. Ray, Fountains of Youth, *Scientific American,* pp. 42-47, August 2000.
7. C. J. Lada and N. D. Kylafis, *The Origins of Stars and Planetary Systems,* Kluwer Academic Publishers, New York, 1999.
8. J. M. Greenberg, The Secrets of Stardust, *Scientific American,* pp. 70-75, December 2000.
9. J. P. Henry, U. G. Briel, and H. Bohringer, The Evolution of Galaxy Clusters, *Scientific American,* pp. 52-57, December 1998.
10. S. Van den Bergh and J. E. Hesser, How the Milky Way Formed, *Scientific American,* pp. 72-78, January 1993.

11. B. Barbuy and A. Renzini, *The Stellar Populations of Galaxies,* Kluwer Academic Publishers, New York, 1992.
12. C. J. Hogan, R. P. Kirshner, and N. B. Suntzeff, Surveying Space-Time with Supernovae, *Scientific American,* pp. 45-51, January 1999.
13. K. Thorne, *Black Holes and Time Warps,* W. W. Norton, New York 1994.
14. S. Hawking, *A Brief History of Time,* Bantam Books, New York, pp. 29-32, 1988.
15. P. J. E. Peebles, *Principles of Physical Cosmology,* Princeton University Press, New Jersey, pp. 227-343, 1993.
16. L. Barnett, *The Universe and Dr. Einstein,* Time Inc. Book Division, Chapter 13, 1962.
17. A. Linde, The Self-Reproducing Inflationary Universe, *Scientific American,* pp. 48-55, November 1994.
18. L. M. Krauss, Cosmological Antigravity, *Scientific American,* pp. 52-59, January 1999.
19. M. D. Lemonick, Adventures in Antigravity, *Time,* p. 54, August 7, 2000.
20. G. Musser and M. Alpert, Brave New Cosmos, *Scientific American,* p. 37, January 2001.
21. J. P. Ostriker and P. J. Steinhardt, Quintessential Universe, *Scientific American,* pp. 46-53, January 2001.
22. L. M. Krauss, Dark Matter in the Universe, *Time,* Understanding Space, pp. 87-97, 1996.
23. B. N. Dwivedi and K. J. H. Phillips, Paradox of the Sun's Hot Corona, *Scientific American,* pp. 40-44, June 2001.
24. J. C. Wheeler, *Cosmic Catastrophes,* Cambridge University Press, New York, 2000.
25. P. Kahabka, E. P. J. van den Heuvel, and S. A. Rappaport, Supersoft X-Ray Stars and Supernovae, *Scientific American,* pp. 46-53, February 1999.
26. M. C. Begelman and M. J. Rees, *Gravity's Fatal Attraction: Black Holes in the Universe,* W. H. Freeman & Co., New York, pp. 130-163, 1998.
27. A. K. Finkbeiner, At the Point of Singularity, *Air & Space,* pp. 70-78, August/September 1993.
28. M. J. Rees, Black Holes in Galactic Centers, *Scientific American,* pp. 56-66, November 1990.
29. M. Schmidt, The Rise and Fall of Quasars, *Highlights of Astronomy, 8,* Kluwer Academic Publishers, New York, 1989.
30. L. Susskind, Black Holes and the Information Paradox, *Scientific American,* pp. 52-57, April 1997.

CHAPTER 9

Why Was I Not Consulted? Where is The Manager?

When someone thinks about life after death, his or her thoughts may drift to religion. Most religions teach that there is an all-powerful, supernatural being that created the universe, and this being guides the destiny of everything in it, including yours and mine. Our destiny is not only about what happens in life, but also after life. Four of the five great religions declare, without any ifs or buts, that the soul or essence of a person is everlasting. The all-powerful, supernatural being has arranged things that way.

Kierkegaard, the Protestant theologian whose questions we have been addressing, considered the concept of God and Christ illogical, yet he accepted them. He accepted them through a "leap of faith" rather than reason. How, he asked, could an all-powerful and kindly God gaze upon the terrible suffering in the world and allow it to go on? If God was omnipotent and kindly as well, why was the suffering permitted to continue? The whole idea of God, he said, was absurd and inconsistent with the facts. It could not be accepted by logic. The obvious paradoxes, such as the concept that Christ was both man and God, could be bridged only by a leap of faith. Faith, and faith alone, made it possible to swallow religion that so defied logic. This was the outlook of Kierkegaard, the existentialist.

The vast majority of people believe in a god and have done so as far back as we know. Religion obviously satisfies a human need, at least up to now. Also, it has formed the underpinning of a belief in life after death. This is the reason that we will take a look at what the five greatest religions have to say about you, me, our existence, and God.

Every society has developed its own ideas on how humans are created, what is their soul, and what will happen to them after death.

The ideas, it should be pointed out, are not the same. Furthermore, many of these ideas change with time as the society itself changes. For example, Luther the Christian rebelled against what he thought were the corrupt practices of the Catholic priests, and launched Protestantism. For similar reasons, Buddha rebelled against the practices of the Hindu religion, and Buddhism emerged as the result. From each new branch or offshoot of a religion, many new branches sprout to satisfy those people with contrasting ideas so that hundreds of denominations arise. The whole picture can get rather complicated. Let me try here, with humble respect, to sort out a few ideas about belief in different Gods.

JUDAISM [1]

One thing that the five great religions agree upon with no argument is that there is a supernatural being that completely controls our existence. This being has the power to do what it wants, when it wants. For the Jews, the supernatural being is represented by Yahweh, the divine entity or God whom they believe made the universe. "In the beginning God created the heavens and the earth," declares Genesis in the first book of the Torah, the earliest Jewish scripture. Since the beginning of the biblical record, the Hebrews believed there was one God only, and He was just, merciful, and loved man. In contrast, the neighboring peoples in Rome, Greece, Syria, Egypt, and Babylonia had many gods, and they were not thought well of. These gods were held in awe, yet not in a respectful way. They were considered by their worshipers to be immoral, vindictive, capricious, and indifferent to mankind. The gods couldn't care less about humans. How unlike Yahweh!

There were many go-betweens or middle-men between the God of the early Jews (Yahweh) and his people. God was able to speak to the people through the biblical prophets and make clear to them exactly what He wanted and what He expected from the human race that he had created. For example, God provided some six hundred and thirteen commandments to be found in the Old Testament exhorting man to be moral, just, and to live in harmony with his fellows. The Jews made an agreement with God called the Covenant. They agreed to serve and suffer in the redemption of the world, and in return God would give them his blessing. The Jews were the people chosen by God to do this. They agreed to do it. That was their Covenant with God.

What do the Jews believe will happen to them when they die? Will they have an existence after death? The books of the Old Testament have very little to say about life after death. There is a place called Sheol first mentioned in the eighth century B.C. and is described in the Old Testament as the underworld home of departed spirits where there is no hope, no joy, only a shadowy existence without thought of punishment or reward. Sort of a pointless, never-never land where nothing good happens, nor anything particularly bad. On the other hand, the Apocalyptic literature which emerged between 200 B.C. and 100 A.D. speaks of both good and bad in the form of paradise or fiery hell, but these writings are looked upon as being contradictory and inconsistent. What about the idea of reincarnation that is so important to some other religions? It has little place in Jewish religious thought. Reincarnation is not mentioned in the Old Testament, although the Talmud, compiled in the early centuries after Christ, contains references to the transmigration of souls. So does the mystical Cabalistic division of Judaism dating from the second century A.D. What, as a rule, do Jews think today about their prospects for life after death? Today, belief in an afterlife by the Jewish people ranges from an absolute conviction held by Orthodox Jews to a more moderate hope on the part of Reform Jews. There appears to be no consensus.

CHRISTIANITY [5-9]

Christians have the same God as Jews, namely Yahweh of the Old Testament. The Christians, however, have a more complicated idea of the supernatural power that created them and the world. The Christian concept of the Trinity holds that, while God is fully one, He is also three. These are respectively God the Father, God the Son, and God the Holy Spirit. Three Gods in one. Since Christians, like Jews, consider themselves to be monotheistic, that is, having only one God, this division into three may seem contrary to logic. The paradox, as noted by Kierkegaard, is compounded when it is understood that Jesus was regarded as a God-man. The Christian doctrine of the Incarnation holds that God assumed a human body, and affirms that Christ was simultaneously both fully God and fully man. Being two different things at once rings a bell in modern physics where it has been noted that, according to quantum experiment, a substance can be simultaneously two things at once: both a wave and a particle. Christians believe that there is something they call the Holy Spirit that is the third God of the Trinity, and the Holy Spirit resides in and animates the human soul. Further, Roman Catholicism holds that, by a life of prayer, the Holy Spirit may disclose its presence to the worshiper and lift him or her to a state of mystical ecstasy.

When it comes to the question of life after death, the Christian belief is that, after death, life enters a supernatural domain. The idea of Salvation is very important here. If a person's soul is "saved," it enters a state of eternal happiness called Heaven. If it is not saved, the soul is likely to exist in a state of punishment called Hell, and will probably stay there forever. It is stated in the Book of Revelation, written almost a century after Christ, that hell is a terrible place that is reserved for all kinds of sinners. It says: "But the fearful, and unbelieving, and the abominable, and murderers, and whoremongers, and sorcerers, and idolaters, and all liars, shall have their part in the lake which burneth with fire and brimstone." However, this scary scenario has little to do with Christ's teaching and may have been written by a questionable fanatic. There is no consistent model of Hell in the Bible. It would seem that hell, the one of fire and brimstone, is a man-made idea.

But Christians do believe in eternal life. Christianity holds that God came to earth in the person of Jesus Christ to teach people how to be saved, pointing out the proper way they should behave in this world in order to have eternal life in the next. Christian belief was not always that way. Such beliefs in the immortality of the soul appear to be late additions to Christian thought, and they are not seen anywhere in the Bible. According to Roman Catholic doctrine, the soul may go to Purgatory instead of Heaven or Hell. Purgatory, not mentioned in the New Testament, was an invention of early Christian Fathers who considered it a place or state of temporary punishment, "where those who have died in the grace of God are expiating their venial faults and such pains as are still due" despite the fact that the sins they committed in life have already been forgiven. Unlike Roman Catholics, Protestants reject the idea of Purgatory. As for reincarnation, most Christian theologians today don't believe in it. However, it should be mentioned as a matter of historical fact that reincarnation was accepted up to the time of the Council of Constantinople that took place five and a half centuries after Christ. Currently, some so-called "New Agers" consider that certain references in the Gospels favor a belief in reincarnation.

HINDUISM [5, 10-12]

Hinduism has its own distinct flavor. Eastern and Western cultures, as we know, are quite different, and their religions are as different as their cultures. Hinduism, the ancient religion of the East, contrasts with Judaism and its offshoots, the religions that have so strongly influenced the West. Extraordinary images of Indian ascetics walking on hot coals or stretched out on beds of nails are perhaps extreme examples that point up differences between the traditional Eastern and Western outlook. It is the attitude, or outlook, that is important here. What the seriously religious Hindu wants is to isolate himself from the physical world, to shut down his senses, to shine the spotlight on his divine interior rather than upon the world outside. The exterior things don't matter. This desire to get away from worldly distractions, to put down material things, is definitely not shared by the Westerner whose bible proclaims: "God saw everything that He made and behold it was very good." For the Westerner, physical aspects of existence are to be relished. Material things count and are an important part of God's creation. Genesis states that man should have dominion over all the earth, and the Westerner believes it, enthusiastically embracing both the material and the spiritual sides of life. This interest in material things contrasts dramatically with the Eastern view in which mankind has no business meddling with nature. The Hindu yogi says: don't mess with material things, concentrate instead on the soul. The yogi wishes to leave things as they are, not to interfere with the natural order around him. His liberation lies ultimately in extricating his spirit from its material environment. The Westerner, on the other hand, has an urge to step in when he sees something askew, to straighten it up, make it right, make things better. God made a Covenant with the ancient Hebrews in which he instructed them to go out and create a just society. The social revolutions and scientific advances so prominent in Western history may well stem from this biblical Covenant in which the God-given role of man was to improve the world.

Who is the God of the Hindus? The name of this supreme being, this ultimate reality for the Hindus, is Brahman. Brahman may be thought of as a personal, compassionate, involved God *Saguna Brahman*, or as a more abstract God *Nirguna Brahman*, who does not get involved with mankind's problems. The former, *Saguna Brahman*, who shows love, mercy, power, and understanding, does get involved. *Saguna Brahman* is commonly regarded as existing in three distinct parts, a parallel with the Christian Trinity concept. These three parts are *Brahma*, who created the universe, *Vishnu*, who preserves it, and *Shiva*, who will take it back. The contemporary philosopher and author, Huston Smith, describes Hinduism's blueprint of the universe: "There would be innumerable galaxies comparable to our own, each focusing in an earth from which men wend their ways to God. Periodically, the cosmos collapses into a Night of *Brahma*, and all phenomenal being is returned to a state of pure potentiality. Thus like a gigantic accordion the world swells out and is drawn back in. This oscillation is a permanent feature of existence; the universe had no beginning and will have no end" [5].

This graphic picture conjures up, for the cosmologist, the idea of Big Bangs alternating with Big Crunches without end. In such a world, the Hindu feels that all talk of social progress is to misconstrue God's purpose which is to provide an arena for the training of the soul.

Although Brahman is worshiped as the one God of the Hindu religion, this God is prayed to using hundreds of physical images and artifacts that help to focus and hold the worshiper's mind on a God that is invisible. God, according to some Hindus, also shows himself in human forms such as Rama, Krishna, Christ, and Buddha.

The rallying point for Hindus is the soul. This is their involvement in existence. Hinduism holds that every individual has a separate soul called the *jiva* which is a person's unique personality. What makes this soul tick is the *Atman,* which is a part of the supreme God, Brahman. Brahman, the *Atman*, lives in the soul although it doesn't always show. The Hindu *yogi's* goal is to dig under those surface layers to reveal and become one with the *Atman* that resides deep within him. He will struggle to ignore pain (bed of nails, red hot coals) and desire which are worldly things, and try only to think of the God within him. Worldly things, he believes, touch only the surface of reality. Limitless joy and serenity are matters of the soul that cannot possibly be ruffled by worldly events which are only temporary. This way of looking at the world would seem to account for the air of calm and settled peace in the eyes and expression of advanced *yogis*, wandering about in simple rags, alms bowl in hand, without the basic comforts of roof or bed. By rejecting worldly pleasures, they have been able to get rid of their egos and find a state of ecstasy unknown to their materially better off brothers. This state may be compared, perhaps, to the mystical heights where a Christian, according to Roman Catholic doctrine, may be transported when the spiritual soul within him or her emerges by reason of a life of constant prayer.

REINCARNATION [13-19]

What does the Hindu religion have to say about life after death? The Hindu is convinced of something that the Jews and Christians are not. It is a major difference between religions. The Hindu believes that, when he or she dies, the soul will depart from the lifeless corpse and enter a newly born body, either that of a human, an animal, or a plant. Note, however, that the soul does not enter the new body immediately, but first must spend a period of time in one of a number of other worlds. Whether the Hindu finds this other world pleasing or not depends on the life that he or she has lived on Earth prior to death.

This idea of rebirth is called reincarnation, and means giving a new physical body to clothe the soul. A long series of rebirths is thought to happen for each individual until the soul, if all goes well, achieves perfection and fuses with God. After this fusion, the individual's soul will remain forever in blissful union with Brahman. No more rebirths, no more suffering. This is the goal of the seriously religious Hindu.

Literally, the word "incarnate" means "in the flesh." Reincarnation denotes something put in the flesh again, that is, given a new body. Actually, in the common usage of the word, reincarnation does not refer to flesh only, for the new body may be a tree, a stone, anything. And what is this "something" that gets a new body and loses an old one? The "something" is what the Hindus call the soul, an eternal spiritual substance whose home on Earth is in a body of material substance. It is said that the soul leaves the old body at death, and passes into another body that has just been born. This process of leaving one body and entering another can be repeated thousands—some say an endless number—of times.

The word reincarnation is often interchanged with other terms such as transmigration, metempsychosis, and palingenesis. They all refer to the passage of the soul through a sequence of bodies. As mentioned, these bodies do not have to be human. In fact, the soul is said to pass through a series of non-human bodies, each one more complex than the last, until finally as a crowning achievement it obtains a human form. Before taking up residence in a human, the soul's growth is considered to be virtually *automatic*. However, once in a human body, the soul reaches self consciousness for the first time. This is an important milestone for the soul. With it comes freedom and also responsibility, because every decision will produce a consequence for which the individual is accountable. The changes that a soul undergoes as it passes from one body to the next is purely the result of its moral choices until, if and when perfection is reached, the soul merges with God and escapes the otherwise endless cycle of rebirths.

Thus, there is a purpose for these multiple rebirths. It is what the Hindus call *karma*. This word, *karma,* refers to an individual's deeds and thoughts during life, and it is these deeds and thoughts which determine what kind of body, and what quality of existence, will be enjoyed or suffered with the next rebirth. "You make your bed and you sleep in it," or "as a man sows, so shall he reap" is the general idea of the whole process. It is said that *karma* is the principle according to which the soul is being continually judged and educated. The consequences of man's past decisions cause his present lot, and his present decisions determine his future. In this way, each individual gets exactly what he deserves and reincarnation is the means by which this purpose is realized. Or so it is thought by something like half the human population of this planet.

BUDDHISM [5, 20, 21]

Most people are familiar with the image of the plump, smiling Buddha. His name is Siddhartha Guatama, the son of well to do parents living in India about twenty-five hundred years ago. Buddha and the sect that he founded reacted against the ritualistic, corrupted state of Hinduism in India at that time. These two great religions of Indian origin, Buddhism and Hinduism, share a common outlook on life. For example, the serious Buddhist monk and the dedicated Hindu *yogi* struggle to reach their religious goals by detaching their minds from the distractions of what they consider the non-real physical world. They try to concentrate only upon what is significant, namely, the reality of the inner being. Buddhism and Hinduism do not differ much with respect to this basic belief in rejecting the external world. However, unlike the Hindu, the Buddhist believes in no personal God. He does not believe in Brahman. Neither does the Buddhist think that he has an individual, immortal soul (atman), nor is his idea of reincarnation the same as that of the Hindu. Finally, another difference may be noted: Buddhism was founded by one individual, Siddhartha Gautama, whereas the roots of Hinduism come from no single person.

What did the Buddha, Gautama, have to say about God? Not much. One of the few references that he made to a supernatural being has been quoted: "There is, O monks, an Unborn, neither become nor created nor formed. . . . Were there not, there would be no deliverance from the born, the made, the compounded." This is perhaps as close as Gautama, in the vast Pali scriptures, comes to offering a concept of God.

Buddha's religion was psychological rather than metaphysical. Gautama dealt with man's problems in the here and now. His teachings were not abstract. He was reluctant to be drawn into any discussion of creation, God, the specifics of an afterlife, or metaphysical concepts. Gautama, instead, concentrated from the beginning upon man, his challenges, his essence, his growth, and resisted discussion of any larger metaphysical picture. However, the state of Nirvana, the enlightened mental condition to which every serious Buddhist aspires, has been described as close enough to the idea of God that it may be thought of as similar to a Godhead. Yet Gautama denied the existence of any God. The literal meaning of Nirvana is extinction, but the Buddhist uses the word to mean extinction of the ego, not the extinction of being.

Gautama said that Nirvana is "incomprehensible, indescribable, inconceivable, unutterable . . . bliss."

It is interesting to note that, despite his denial of God, Gautama himself came to be known as God within some sects of Buddhism.

How about the soul? Did the Buddha have anything to say about the soul? Yes, but in a negative way. In his teaching, Gautama said that man doesn't have a soul that holds its distinct nature eternally. He thus did not agree with the Hindus who thought that there exists an individual *Atman*, or divine soul, which is destined ultimately to be reunited with Brahman, or God. The concept of a changeless *Atman*, one that has no beginning or end, which forms the basic essence of each of us, clearly contrasts with Gautama's *anatta*, or no soul, doctrine.

When the Buddha, Gautama, was asked what happens at death to the individual who, in life, has attained to Nirvana, he fudged. His replies were mysterious so that people put different meanings to them. The nearest we can come to knowing what the Buddha thought about the final destiny of the human spirit is that all identification with the finite, earthly self *and its memories* will be lost, while experience itself will remain and find itself augmented beyond human capacity to imagine. In other words, the human will have no recollection of his or her past life or identity, but will nevertheless experience after death a greater existence than can be imagined in this life. The fact that several centuries elapsed after the Buddha's death before his remembered words were set down in literary form must surely have scrambled to some unknown degree the accuracy and precision of his recorded views on spirit life. One of the Buddha's disciples is reported to have said:

> Whether the world is eternal or not eternal, whether the world is finite or not, whether the soul is the same as the body or whether the soul is one thing and the body another, whether a Buddha exists after death or does not exist after death—these things the Lord (Gautama) does not explain to me.

With regard to reincarnation that is so central to the Hindu religion, the Buddhist doctrine, as conceived by Gautama, seems more vague and contradictory than that of the Hindus. Gautama denied the Hindu notion of a soul that passes from one body to another, but accepted the Hindu concept of *karma* which holds that the deeds of one life are instrumental in the shaping of the subsequent life. Although Buddhism asserts that there is no self, or historical memory link, that remains intact through any series of rebirths, we are faced with the paradox that Gautama himself, and other enlightened *Arhats* that succeeded him, claim to remember the events of thousands of their past lives. The "logical" Western mind groans and boggles when it tries to grasp and reconcile these seemingly illogical and irreconcilable contradictions.

ISLAM [5, 22-24]

Islam! The very word conjures up images in the minds of some Westerners of fanatical, unruly mobs, religious ruffians, a rude, inscrutable culture practicing cruel, primitive justice. This is simply not true. It may, indeed, have been the case in Mecca before the sixth century A.D. as it was in many other parts of the world at that time. But the birth of Mohammed, the founder of Islam, about 571 A.D. changed Arab society enormously through his preaching of rigorous moral behavior and orderly conduct.

It is seldom recognized by Westerners that Islam and Christianity share a lot in common. For example, both have their roots in the religion of the Jews, Judaism, and both point to the biblical figure of Abraham as a common ancestor. Muslims and Christians, alike, hold sacred the ten commandments handed down to Moses as a model for human conduct, and both religions advocate a moral code of love and justice which is written in their scriptures, the Koran and the Bible.

What is it that sets these great religions, Islam and Christianity, apart, that makes the devout Muslim and the serious Christian different in their religious conduct? The main difference, perhaps, involves the much stricter code of behavior that is required of the Muslim by the Koran. This word of God, delivered to the Prophet Mohammed and written down by Mohammed's followers, did not leave to chance or philosophical debate how each and every Muslim was to pray, dress, eat, and live. God spelled it all out, dotting the i's and crossing the t's. The Koran states exactly what each Muslim must, and must not, do in order to live a righteous life and attain Paradise. The Christian Bible, on the contrary, is more flexible. It gives wider license to individual discretion with regard to the manner in which God's wishes are to be fulfilled. How many wives may a man take? Jesus didn't say, but Mohammed mentioned four. How should the poor be treated? The Bible says generously, but the Koran specifies 2½ percent of a man's wealth annually must be given to the poor. How often should one pray to God? Frequently, advocated Christ, whereas Mohammed was more precise, stipulating five times a day, at certain periods of the day, and in a specific way facing Mecca.

Who is the God of the Muslims? About this there is no doubt. The devout Muslim cries out over the rooftops loud and clear for all the world to hear: "There is no God but Allah, and Mohammed is his Prophet."

Well, what about the God of the Christians? Is the Christian deity the same God that the Muslim is proclaiming? This tricky question has long been debatable. The Christian worshiper will argue that he, too, is monotheistic and worships only one God, the God of Abraham and Moses, the Yahweh of Judaism. "Ah, but," counters the Muslim, "that God happens to be our God, Allah." "Maybe so," replies the Christian, "but it has been revealed to us that He is really three, a Trinity. And by the way, one of those three is Jesus, the Son of God." "Nonsense," says the Muslim. "Allah has no Son! Allah is the supreme and only divinity, the almighty Creator, undivided, one. We grant you that Jesus was an important Prophet like Mohammed, but definitely not divine. There is no God but Allah." And so the controversy goes.

On the question of soul, there is considerable agreement between the Christian and the Muslim. When the devout Muslim thinks about the soul, the image that comes to his mind is similar to that which comes to the mind of his Christian cousin. The human soul, says Islam, was created by an act of God's will, and represents God's supreme accomplishment. It is the essence of man's being, and once created, the individual soul is without end in time. Both the Koran and the Bible disclose a high regard for the soul as an expression of man's individuality. This contrasts with the scriptures of Eastern religions that downplay the importance of man's individual personality or separateness. The Easterners, in fact, regard the personality as an impediment to mankind's ability to comprehend reality.

Now, what about the Muslim's view of life after death? It is quite straightforward. The Koran teaches that, on the day of Judgment after death, each individual will be accountable for the way he has lived. There is a narrow bridge that crosses over hell to paradise. If the dead candidate has led a wicked life and is judged wanting, he will fall off the bridge into hell and be subject to everlasting torment. If he is, on the other hand, judged worthy, he will reach paradise and, according to Mohammed, ". . . see his Lord's face night and morning. . . ." This concept of man's destiny is not unlike that of the Roman Catholic Christian who, according to Maurice and Louis Becque, at the moment of death when the soul separates from the body, is accorded a judgment that is marked by two qualities and dispositions: "it is irrevocable and it is immediate . . . heaven, purgatory, or hell."

What, then, is the Muslim's view of heaven? According to the Koran, it abounds in deep rivers of cool, crystal water, lush fruit and vegetables, boundless fertility, and beautiful mansions with gracious attendants. One can imagine that these images of water and green growth would be especially attractive to the Arab used to scuffling for basic sustenance in the dry, barren desert. We hear about religious Muslims willingly sacrificing themselves in car bombs or minefields for such instant rewards in heaven. However, if the Muslim has any doubts about his ability to cross the bridge to paradise, he may wish to think twice about contracting for a premature passage to hell which Islam describes for him as a scalding crater of molten metal, boiling liquids, and fire. These images would be particularly repellent to the Arab, perhaps, who spends a lifetime battling the heat of sun and sand. With regard to this vivid imagery of heaven and hell, it is written in the Koran that some of the signs are firm, some are figurative.

Does the Muslim believe in Purgatory? Yes, the Koran speaks of a kind of intermediary place situated between the pleasures of paradise and the torments of hell where those who were neither good nor wicked will go. The Roman Catholic concept of Purgatory, by comparison, is a state where the guilty actions of a person's life may be completely effaced after death before that person goes to heaven . Does the Muslim believe, like the Hindu, in the reincarnation of the soul in a series of innumerable rebirths on earth? No. Like Christians, the vast majority of Muslims reject such theories. Neither do the Muslims, unlike the Christians, accept the concept that God was incarnated on earth in the form of Jesus Christ. They accept the historical fact of Jesus as a man and a prophet of God, but consider it naive to suppose that he was God made into flesh.

CONTRASTING VIEWS OF THE SOUL

Maybe we can have ourselves a little fun at this point by seeing how the author's Saved Consciousness Hypothesis fits into thousands of years of religious history.

Suppose you ask somebody: "What is the soul?" The answer you get would probably depend on that person's religion. You could expect the Theravadan Buddhist to answer: "There is no such thing as a soul." This is Buddha's *anatta* (no soul) doctrine.

Now, a Hindu *yogi*, if he overheard this, would likely smile wryly and shake his head in gentle disapproval. Traditional Hindu thought regards individual human souls (*jivas*) as having existed through unlimited time, sooner or later, after countless reincarnations, to be united with God.

Let us suppose that, as the Hindu wanders off seeking alms, you approach a Christian and a Muslim who, by chance, are strolling together, and you ask them: "What is the soul?" Either one might reply to this effect: "The soul is the essence of the human being, created by God, destined to be immortal. If the individual has led a moral life, the soul, with a new spiritual body, ultimately enters a state of eternal happiness in the presence of God. If the individual, instead, has committed evil deeds and not repented, the soul may spend eternity in a state of punishment." Neither the Christian nor the Muslim has anything to say about multiple reincarnations of the soul on earth.

Finally, let us suppose that you encounter a pedestrian who clutches a copy of this book, *Prospects for Immortality,* in his hand. You assume from this that he may be an advocate of the Saved Consciousness Hypothesis, and you ask him: "What is the soul?" He glances at the Christian and Muslim still loitering nearby, clears his throat, and replies: "If by 'soul' you refer to the Self, that is, the sense of self awareness that every individual has, then the soul is what survives the death of the body. In its new multidimensional environment, the soul may acquire a new body (nothing like the old one) that is adapted to and able to interact with its new environment. One can further speculate that the soul could find itself in community with other post mortem 'souls' quite able to continue the soul growth that was begun on earth and which makes of it an increasingly complex entity." Having delivered himself of these pearls, the advocate of saved consciousness moves off in search of the author of his book in order to get it autographed.

If we stand and ponder these various viewpoints, we can find no universal consensus. The Buddhist says no soul, period. The Hindu says yes, there is a soul perfected through multiple rebirths on earth and then merged in bliss with the eternal Brahman. Wrong, say the Christian and Muslim, there are no rebirths because the soul, if it eludes Satan, rises to the eternal joy of a supernatural domain where, before God, it is further perfected. The saved consciousness advocate hedges. He will only say that there are rational grounds to believe that the Self could survive death by re-living life, and possibly continue to develop in a new milieu. The delicate thread of agreement that is shared by the Hindu, Christian, Muslim, and Saved Consciousness advocate relates to the existence of a soul, its immortality, and its ongoing evolution. The Buddhist does not concur with any of these concepts.

ANTICIPATING DEATH

Although we all anticipate that we will die sooner or later, is this any reason to dwell on it? We live in the present, the here and now, so what good does it do to morbidly reflect on death? When it's over, it's over, the fat lady sings, and that's that. What is due to happen will happen, and there is little we can do about it. Right?

Wrong, says religion. The here and now is less than a drop of water in the Pacific Ocean, less than a grain of sand in the Sahara Desert. By contrast, Eternity is forever, a timeless existence that lies before us. The bottom line is this: what we do in this life will determine the way we spend that infinite eternity after we die. Let's take a closer look at this idea and its obvious importance, if true, for each one of us. Let's compare some different viewpoints on life after death.

You will remember that, a few paragraphs back, we imagined you asking a Buddhist, a Christian, a Muslim, and an advocate of saved consciousness, what they thought about the soul. Suppose now that the Christian to whom you spoke is standing across the street leafing through a copy of the New Testament.

You go up to him and ask: "What happens to us when we die?"

The Christian does not hesitate: "We go," he answers, "to Heaven, Purgatory, or Hell. Catholics go to Purgatory, some of them, but it is only temporary. If you believe in Christ and keep the Sacraments and the moral law, it's directly to Heaven, for sure."

The Muslim, fingering his Koran, has overheard the conversation, and joins the group. "It's true what the Christian says," he declares, "except the part about the Sacraments and Christ. Jesus was not a God. There is only one God, Allah."

The Hindu, who has had no luck seeking alms for his empty bowl, now approaches and quietly intones: "There are many other higher and lower realms or planes of existence in which souls can live between reincarnations. In these heavenly, purgatorial, or hellish spheres, the soul reaps the consequences of good or evil deeds done in this world." He pauses to smile indulgently. "But, gentlemen, it is only in the physical body, on earth, that the soul is able to undergo further stages of development toward the ultimate self awareness that we call *moksha*."

"You are mistaken there," says the Christian. "Irenaean theology clearly states that the soul-making process extends beyond this earthly scene to other supernatural worlds."

"Well, I disagree with that," rejoins the Hindu. "And by the way, there is no permanent hell and no eternal damnation."

The Muslim jumps in: "That is where you are wrong, sir. Check your Koran."

A passing Orthodox Jew, who has picked up on some of the remarks, stops long enough to thumb rapidly through the Torah. He announces: "There is nothing in here specifically about Heaven or Hell. When you die, gentlemen, you go to Sheol. That is a shadowy sort of place, no fun, a rotten experience. I hope I don't go."

The others remain silent, so the Jew turns on his heel and leaves. The Christian speaks to the Muslim: "Never mind about the rabbi. I agree with this Hindu chap about further stages of soul development. But reincarnation is nonsense. The development occurs in Heaven. Remember, Jesus said, 'In the house of the Father, there are many Mansions.'"

He turns to direct a meaningful glance at the Hindu, but that *yogi*, seeing a prospect for alms, has left. A clock is heard striking noon, and the Muslim drops to his prayer rug. The Christian, left alone, decides to say a few Hail Mary's, then departs.

Now, what might the saved consciousness advocate have contributed to this verbal interchange if he had been present? Would he have had any relevant views? Let's imagine that the Christian, Muslim, Hindu, and Jew have met once more, and are being addressed by the advocate of saved consciousness.

Advocate: "Gentlemen, your ideas on death and the hereafter are interesting, but fanciful. The book which I hold here in my hand is more realistic, I submit, than your scriptures. It deals with how we get from here to there. Unfortunately, it is not yet autographed."

Jew: "What does it say, already?"

Advocate: "It postulates that consciousness is saved. You can get the details from chapters 2 and 5, so I won't bother you with them here. The bottom line is this: consciousness in life is a series of voltage waves in the brain which are all transported to the hereafter."

The Advocate looks from face to face to measure the effect of his words. The Muslim stares back at him.

Muslim: "There is only one God, Allah, and His prophet is Mohammed!"

Advocate: "Maybe so, sir, but let me ask you this. Have you ever heard of the expression 'You can't take it with you'? Well, it's wrong! You can jolly well take your consciousness with you."

Christian: "Says who?"

Advocate: "The hypothesis of saved consciousness. It's all explained in this book."

Christian: "Sounds like gibberish."

Muslim: "There is only one God. . . ."

The Advocate holds up his hand.

Advocate: "The consciousness of your past life is the only thing you take with you when you die. This makes you accountable. Don't you see? If the memories are evil, you carry your own hell as baggage. If they are good, you have created your own heaven."

Christian: "Nonsense. When, and if, you get to Heaven, you will have a new existence in the presence of God."

Advocate: "Possibly, yes, but. . . ."

Muslim: "I say to you all, there is only one God, Allah. . . ."

Advocate: "Yes, yes, possibly . . . but, regardless, you will relive your past consciousness on Earth over and over, like the reincarnations of our Hindu friend here."

The Hindu, who has been rocking gently on the balls of his bare feet while making unobtrusive snoring noises, opens an eye and leers at the Advocate.

Hindu: "What *yogi* says your book is right?"

Advocate: "No *yogi*. It is not a religion. But the hypothesis in this book, whose author I'm trying to locate. . . . The hypothesis, I say, is obviously based on fact, not fancy."

Jew: "Sounds off the wall to me."

Advocate: "No, sir. Even your shadowy Sheol could be a garbled replay of some bad dreams which are a form of consciousness."

Jew: "Where, might I ask, is this alleged consciousness located? It must exist somewhere, certainly not in the dead person's head?"

The Hindu, who has been meditating upon reincarnation, is now wide awake, and speaks with missionary zeal.

Hindu: "It is on earth, that's where! It is reborn on earth. The soul, as we all know, is transferred into a newborn body of flesh."

The Jew peers at the Hindu, then turns to the Advocate.

Jew: "Do you buy that?"

Advocate: "Well, no. This Hindu chap needs the doctrine of reincarnation to back up his idea of karma. He thinks that past wrongs are ultimately made right through a series of rebirths on earth. No, I don't buy it, nor do I believe in the tooth fairy."

Christian: "Then do you believe that the soul reaches perfection through stages? And if so, where?"

Advocate: "I believe it may. What you call the soul I prefer to think of as self-awareness. As to where it is transferred, the hypothesis in this book suggests a possible milieu; namely, the subatomic dimensions of quantum physics. We have a glimmer of evidence that they exist, that they are multiple, that they are unusual, and mysterious. And here is a point I would like to make, gentlemen. We are not dealing here with a supernatural, never-never land of the imagination. The quantum world is quite real with measurable parameters."

Jew: "As I said before, the theory sounds off the wall to me."

Advocate: "May I correct you, Sir. Saved consciousness is no theory, only a hypothesis. It will remain pure speculation until tested."

Muslim: "It is not in the Koran."

Jew: "Nor in the Torah."

Hindu: "It's not written in the Upanishads, nor have I seen it in the Bhagavad Gita."

Christian: "I can tell you for sure its not mentioned in the Bible."

The Advocate of saved consciousness smirks and prepares to leave.

Advocate: "Gentlemen, the ideas that I share with you today have neither been verified, nor falsified. The case for saved consciousness rests on rational assumptions, I can say no more. You might want to get hold of a copy of this book."

The motley group, looking skeptical to a man, disperses while wondering if it would be an act of heresy to read such a volume. The Advocate, for his part, has heard that the author may be found quaffing ale at a local watering hole around the corner, and repairs thence post haste for a possible autograph.

REFERENCES

1. M. Steinberg, *Basic Judaism,* Harcourt, Brace & Co., New York, 1947.
2. A. L. Sachar, *History of the Jews,* Knopf, New York, 1953.
3. W. Irwin, *The Old Testament: Keystone of Human Culture,* Schuman, New York, 1952.

4. G. E. Wright, *The Old Testament Against Its Environment,* Allenson, Chicago, 1951.
5. H. Smith, *The Religions of Man,* Harper Perennial, New York, 1986.
6. P. Ramsey, *Basic Christian Ethics,* Charles Scribner's Sons, New York, 1952.
7. R. Knox, *The Creed in Slow Motion,* Sheed and Ward, London, 1949.
8. T. Corbishley, *Roman Catholicism,* Longmans and Green, New York, 1950.
9. J. Dillenberger and C. Welch, *Protestant Christianity Interpreted Through Its Development,* Charles Scribner's Sons, New York, 1954.
10. Sir S. Radhakrishnan, *The Hindu View of Life,* Macmillan Press, New York, 1927.
11. S. Nikhilananda, *The Essence of Hinduism,* Beacon Press, Boston, 1948.
12. S. Nikhilananda, *The Upanishads* (Vols. 1, 2, 3), Harper & Brothers, New York, 1949, 1952, 1956.
13. A. Berger and J. Berger, *Reincarnation: Fact or Fable?* The Aquarian Press, London, 1991.
14. I. Stevenson, *Twenty Cases Suggestive of Reincarnation,* American Society for Psychical Research, New York, 1966.
15. R. Moody, *Life After Life,* Mockingbird Books, Georgia, 1975.
16. J. Hick, *Death and Eternal Life,* Collins, London, 1976.
17. G. MacGregor, *Images of Afterlife,* Paragon House, New York, 1992.
18. G. Doore, *What Survives?* Jeremy P. Tarcher, California, 1990.
19. J. Algeo, *Reincarnation Explored,* Theosophical Publishing House, Illinois, 1989.
20. J. B. Pratt, *The Pilgrimage of Buddhism and a Buddhist Pilgrimage,* Macmillan, New York, 1928.
21. E. Conze, *Buddhism: Its Essence and Development,* Coronet Books Inc., Pennsylvania, 1999.
22. A. Ali, *The Spirit of Islam,* Christophers, London, 1922.
23. P. Hitti, *The Arabs: A Short History,* Princeton University Press, New Jersey, 1949.
24. K. Cragg, *The Call of the Minaret,* Oxford University Press, New York, 1956.

CHAPTER 10

A Chat with Kierkegaard

The Author of *Prospects for Immortality* sits in a small tavern, quaffing ale from his tankard and quietly contemplating a pretty waitress's shapely legs. A stranger, perhaps in his late thirties, approaches the Author's table and sits down.

"May I join you?" queries the stranger with a pleasant smile.

"You already have," replies the Author.

"My name is Soren Kierkegaard."

"And mine," says the Author, "is Napoleon Bonaparte."

"But you are not Napoleon Bonaparte."

"And you are not Soren Kierkegaard. He's dead."

"Indeed, Sir, I am Soren Kierkegaard."

The stranger extracts a dog-eared copy of *Prospects for Immortality* from a capacious pocket and explains:

"Your publisher told me I might find you here."

"My publisher?" The Author's eyebrows twitch.

"Yes, Baywood. Please don't be alarmed." The stranger held up the book. "I took the liberty of contacting your publisher. I wanted to know where I might find you." He winks. "A young female secretary was most helpful."

The Author, bemused but playing the game, responds.

"Young secretary. That would probably be Janis. What can I do for you? Would you like the book autographed?"

"No Sir. I would like to discuss your book with you. That is why I am here."

The Author scrutinizes the man. "If, my friend, you are *the* Kierkegaard, then you have been dead for a hundred and fifty years."

The stranger hitches his chair a shade closer and peers into the Author's eyes.

"I'm afraid I can't go into that. I am not at liberty to discuss my death." He takes a draught of ale from the tankard that, courtesy of the Author, has appeared in front of him. "Now," says the self-proclaimed Kierkegaard, "May I bother you with some questions I have prepared?"

"Absolutely," responds the Author. "No bother at all." He smiles at the stranger, refreshes himself with a swallow of brown fluid, and enters the following dialogue.

* * *

KIERKEGAARD: Do you think there is life after death?

AUTHOR: You should know.

KIERKEGAARD: But in your opinion, Sir?

AUTHOR: It's possible.

KIERKEGAARD: How? You've explained it in your book, but I would like to hear it directly from your lips.

AUTHOR: By shifting memory and consciousness to another space. Making them independent of the brain.

KIERKEGAARD: But they are dependent on the brain.

AUTHOR Yes, they start in the brain. They are originally generated there, but they don't have to stay in the brain.

KIERKEGAARD: Do you mean to download them to a computer?

AUTHOR: No. That would be impossible. Computers are still very limited, and anyway, how could you make the transfer? Nobody's anywhere near that.

KIERKEGAARD: Then what are you proposing to do?

AUTHOR: I'm not proposing to do anything. I'm saying that consciousness is already being transferred without us doing anything. Automatically. Consciousness, I believe, consists of voltage changes. Electricity in the brain. A series of consecutive voltage changes that have found a final common pathway. We could hook up this pathway to a very sensitive oscilloscope and see the wave. You'd have to find the locus first, and amplify it.

KIERKEGAARD: I don't follow you. What's this got to do with life after death?

AUTHOR: The wave can be stored, or recorded if you will, elsewhere.

KIERKEGAARD: How do you do that?

AUTHOR: You don't. It's being done automatically.

KIERKEGAARD: Where is it being stored?

AUTHOR: Ah! Okay. Do you understand me when I say that the wave is first generated in the brain, but that it can be transferred?

KIERKEGAARD: But transferred where?

AUTHOR: That, of course, is the key question. Well, if you read my book, you know my hypothesis is that the wave is transmitted to subatomic space.

KIERKEGAARD: Where is that?

AUTHOR: Well, do you know anything about quantum theory?

KIERKEGAARD: I have spent the last week in the library. That is where I came across your book. I learn quickly.

AUTHOR: Okay. Then maybe you know that subatomic space has different rules than macroscopic space. Things that happen there are kind of weird.

KIERKEGAARD: How is consciousness transferred to subatomic space?

AUTHOR: It doesn't have to go far. After all, subatomic space co-exists with macroscopic space in the brain. Space is space. An atom is mostly space. If, as you say, you learn fast, then you already know that.

KIERKEGAARD: You're saying that consciousness remains in the brain but in a different space?

AUTHOR: Not really a different space, but in a space that operates by different rules, quantum rules. That's what happens in subatomic space.

Both parties pause in their discussion. The waitress with the pretty legs is summoned, and their tankards are refilled. Kierkegaard scrapes off the excess foam from the rim.

KIERKEGAARD: This space, you say, operates by different rules. It is subatomic space, meaning smaller than an atom. Am I understanding you correctly, Sir?

AUTHOR: You are.

KIERKEGAARD: What does consciousness do in subatomic space?

AUTHOR: It is recorded there. I prefer the word embedded. When we die, consciousness can be played back, or recycled. It's life all over again. I liken it to a magnetic tape on a recording machine being played back.

KIERKEGAARD: But surely there is no magnetic tape in subatomic space?

AUTHOR: Agreed. It is only an analogy. My hypothesis, which is tentative of course, postulates that there is some kind of field analogous to an electromagnetic field.

The speaker notices that his listener's eyes have lost their concentration, so he orders more ale. Both parties restore their tissues with a draught or two.

KIERKEGAARD: You're going a little too fast for me. You say that the voltage wave of consciousness in your brain—have I got it right? is recorded in subatomic space. In what subatomic space? Please try to be clear.

AUTHOR: The subatomic space in your brain. Your brain is mostly space, you know.

KIERKEGAARD: And is this wave, as you call it, recorded continuously? Is the recording taking place without you knowing it? As you're living your life?

AUTHOR: You've got it.

KIERKEGAARD: I have?

AUTHOR: You have.

KIERKEGAARD: What happens if your brain blows up? There goes the consciousness wave! The recording has been for nothing.

AUTHOR: Not at all. You can't destroy space. Your brain is gone, but the space remains. Look, we're talking about a field here. Think of a field, like a gravitational field. You can set off a hydrogen bomb in space, but the gravitational field remains. You don't blow up gravity.

KIERKEGAARD: Humph.

AUTHOR: Your consciousness voltage wave is embedded in a subatomic field and remains there no matter what happens to your brain. I don't know much about your past consciousness, Mr. Kierkegaard. If you want to get rid of it, you can't. It's permanently recorded.

KIERKEGAARD: Are you talking about one's past consciousness, the day-to-day awareness of life as it happened?

AUTHOR: Sure. This transfer goes on from birth to death.

KIERKEGAARD: And it's played back, you say?

AUTHOR: I propose that it's available for playback after death. Actually, regeneration is a better word than playback, I think.

They both pause for thought and Kierkegaard slowly blows the froth around in the top of his glass until it laps at the edges. He wonders where the Author got such unusual ideas.

KIERKEGAARD: Consciousness is a very complex thing to be transferred. I don't think it can be done.

AUTHOR: Sure it can. Look at a Beethoven symphony. It's complex. You can put a Beethoven symphony on a single wire, feed it to a loud speaker, and hear it back. Accurately. High fidelity stuff.

KIERKEGAARD: Consciousness is private, personal. Not at all like music over a loudspeaker that everyone can hear. Your private consciousness cannot be shared by others.

AUTHOR: Ah, but consciousness is not played over a loudspeaker. It is played inside your head. It's played over the earphones of your brain.

Kierkegaard knits a puzzled brow and wags a shaggy head.

KIERKEGAARD: I don't really get it. Why bother with the transfer at all? Why wasn't consciousness created directly in subatomic space in the first place? Who needs a brain?

AUTHOR: A brain is necessary. What we are conscious of in life is our experience in ordinary space. We need our brain for that. Our experiences can't go to subatomic space without first being processed in the brain. And, of course, the brain's connected to the senses, which are necessary to feed information to the brain.

KIERKEGAARD: Well, supposing you are right, how is consciousness restored after death?

AUTHOR: I described that in my book, although you may question it. It is a playback, a regeneration, of your consciousness wave.

KIERKEGAARD: Yes, but playback to whom, and how?

AUTHOR: To itself. Sounds funny? We are looking at an enclosed process. You have what I call a subjective black box in your brain that you are using right now, and you also have one that is quite separate from the one in your brain and it is in quantum space. The box in your brain processes the consciousness wave in your brain, which is the final common pathway of the senses and memory, and somehow turns it into subjective awareness. The box in quantum space will do that when you're dead. Am I muddling you?

KIERKEGAARD: You are.

AUTHOR: Let me try again. This is my postulate. Objective consciousness is a voltage wave, subjective consciousness is something else. There is a subjective box that translates the objective wave into a feeling of awareness, and this happens both in the brain and in subatomic space. But only after death in subatomic space.

The Author clears his throat, lubricates his tonsils with a swallow of ale, nearly chokes and recovers. He smiles at the stranger, and quizzes him.

AUTHOR: Why are you asking *me* all this stuff? You are the one that's supposed to be dead. It's me that should be asking you.

KIERKEGAARD: On the contrary, my feelings are all subjective. I am not a scientist. I am aware only of what I feel subjectively. I know nothing about the mechanism that is responsible for my impressions. I would like to know. You tease me. You have said in your book that this alleged consciousness wave can be recycled, or played back, after death. One wonders what the point would be of recycling past experiences? If we can talk about purpose, what purpose would it have?

AUTHOR: Yes, one wonders. It's not my business to talk about purpose, but nevertheless, I can visualize a benefit. It provides an attachment to our past identity. How else would we recognize ourselves? The identity that we know is the result of our past experiences. Recycling would form a bridge, a continuity between our experiences before and after death. You should know, Kierkegaard. You are the one that is dead, remember?

KIERKEGAARD: You too may be dead.

AUTHOR: I am certainly not.

KIERKEGAARD: You may, even as we speak, be recycling a consciousness wave of your past life. If I read correctly in your book, you say that a person recycling a consciousness wave might think that he or she is actually alive.

The author nods. He has no response for this. He smiles, slowly sips his ale, and nearly chokes again.

AUTHOR: You've got me there, my lad. Maybe I'm dead and recycling.

KIERKEGAARD: You talk about continuity, the Self continuing after death in an ongoing awareness. Why? Your self-awareness disappears in life when you faint or fall into a coma. Why should your consciousness not disappear in death too?

AUTHOR: "Why" is a purpose question. I can't handle purpose questions. Anyway, I will respond. In life you can faint, but when you regain consciousness, you simply carry on where you left off. You don't know you fainted, except that you are lying on the floor. Your subjective awareness resumes exactly at the point where it was before you fainted. No? Why not the same thing in death? When you die, you might lose consciousness for a period of time, but not know it. A billion years could go by with no consciousness, but you would not know this. There would be no awareness of the time lapse. You would continue with your thoughts after the lapse as though no time gap had occurred. Just like when you faint.

KIERKEGAARD: You mean you'd start recycling your old life after a billion years of nothingness?

AUTHOR: Why not?

KIERKEGAARD: Is your Hypothesis only about recycling?

AUTHOR: Yes. But I'm not saying that recycling is the only thing that happens to a person after death. I'm not saying that at all. All kinds of things may happen that I know nothing about. How could I possibly know? I'm simply saying that recycling may form part of an identity bridge. You preserve your past life, and may add that life to a new one about which we have no information. You should know something about that, Mr. Kierkegaard, if you are really Mr. Kierkegaard.

The stranger ignores this personal remark, and seizes upon another point.

KIERKEGAARD: You are talking now about recycling consciousness, or the consciousness wave as you call it. What about the memory banks in your brain? You have mentioned in your book that these form a physical pattern of nerves and synapses, quite a concrete thing. You say that this pattern of memories is also transplanted to subatomic space.

AUTHOR: That is correct. You've got it right. My hypothesis states that they are duplicated there during every moment you live. They also form a bridge to your identity, but there is a difference here. Your trans-located memory patterns contain information that, possibly, you can select at will, as you do in life. In life, you probe your memory bank when you want to remember something. In death, you can choose to probe your memories in the same way, providing that you have a new life in addition to the old one. Something to probe the old memories with. A new consciousness that you can use to ferret out old memories. That's a big presumption, isn't it? You can see that recalling memories of your former life is quite different to reliving your former life by recycling your old consciousness. That's the distinction between your transplanted memories and your transplanted consciousness. Memories are a fixed resource. Consciousness is a sequential process. Get it?

KIERKEGAARD: Well, how could these fixed memory patterns be transported to subatomic space?

AUTHOR: I haven't a clue. It is only a conjecture. The nerve networks of memory in the brain consist of patterns of information, and any pattern of information has the potential for being relocated elsewhere. As Norbert Weiner said.

KIERKEGAARD: Quite a conjecture.

AUTHOR: A massive conjecture.

KIERKEGAARD: What is the main point that you wish to convey with your book?

AUTHOR: The main point is this. We know that we are going to die. The body's atoms and molecules go back to the pool where they came from. Ashes to ashes, as they say. But not consciousness. My Hypothesis says that our past experiences are retained in a permanent form, and the book sketches out a possible mechanism of how this might take place. I agree that it's only a sketch, kind of loose and incomplete. But the nucleus is there.

KIERKEGAARD: You give no evidence.

AUTHOR: There is none. Speculation, my dear Kierkegaard. Nothing proved, but nothing disproved either. One starts with a guess.

KIERKEGAARD: I suppose. But why nominate the subatomic world, of all places, for post-mortem existence?

AUTHOR: Infinite capacity for storage, part of our universe, contiguous with the brain.

KIERKEGAARD: Does your hypothesis propose that one is immediately conscious after death?

AUTHOR: Well, we spoke about that, but let's go over it again. Subjectively, yes, we would think we were immediately conscious. As soon as the playback began. But who knows, it might not begin for a million years. We would not be aware of this gap. As far as we were concerned, there would be no absence of consciousness. I am talking about consciousness of the old life. A new life is something else. There is no information on that. A new life after death is so far only in our imagination.

KIERKEGAARD: An interesting idea, Sir. Let me ask a slightly different question. Are animals conscious like us, and do they retain consciousness after death? I forget if you mention this in your book.

AUTHOR: I do, and I did mention it. Or if I didn't, I should have. We are animals. Presumably the same forces that act upon our memories and consciousness would act upon those of other animals. We will be conscious again of our happy and painful moments. So will they. The thing to remember, of course, is that there are different degrees of complexity in the brains of different animals. Look, a worm has only a few rudimentary ganglia for a central nervous system. There is far less processing power there. It's certainly not going to have the same consciousness wave that we humans have.

KIERKEGAARD: I shall have to ask you again about the distinction you make between memory and consciousness. Please forgive me, but I am not quite clear on this. Are memories and consciousness not more or less the same thing?

AUTHOR: Not at all. They are not the same thing although they overlap and are interconnected. Here is the difference. The memory is composed of a very large number of nerves and their connections which are all hard-wired in the brain. The nerves are in a definite pattern. Norbert Weiner pointed out fifty years ago, and he was right in my opinion, that any pattern can be sent to another place and copied there, using the same or different materials. He called it telegraphing. We have evidence for this.

KIERKEGAARD: I find it hard to visualize.

AUTHOR: Think of a pattern, say the pattern of a maze in a kid's puzzle book. The pattern—note I say the pattern, not the ink—can be moved to another place, let's say electronically, without moving the original maze itself. So can music on a disk be transmitted electronically to another place without moving the disk itself. You are simply sending the pattern of the grooves or magnetic information electronically to another place. Why not brain memory too? Why can't the brain telegraph the pattern of its nerve network to another place without itself moving? I have postulated that this is what is actually happening during life with memory. The pattern of the nerve network is telegraphed, as Weiner would say, to subatomic space. That's the case for memory. That's what also happens to consciousness, but the two are separate and distinct. One is a static maze, the other is a dynamic wave.

KIERKEGAARD: What would memory do in subatomic space?

AUTHOR: Ha! This is where we get into pure fantasy. I have already spoken about this. I can only propose that our transplanted memory would be available to whatever new post mortem existence we might be blessed with apart from recycling. Both consciousness and memory would maintain our identity for us. With memory, though, you've got a different situation. In the case of memory, the things you remember would *not* have to follow one another as they originally did in life. They would not have to be in their original sequence. They would be available to you in a new afterlife, if such exists, on the basis of voluntary selection just like they are in this life. Sort of like books in a library that you pick out as you need them. The consciousness wave is different. It is your past life run in sequence, more like a movie film than a library. But I would like to stress something that I have repeated several times before, and probably will do again. It is this. In the case of recycling, you're not just watching your old life, you're re-living it. You are re-doing exactly what you did in the past and are aware of it in exactly the same way that you were in the past. There is no distinction, as far as you're concerned, between the recycled and the original.

KIERKEGAARD: I think I get your point. You regard trans-planted memory, quite distinct from consciousness, as a library of books where, in a new life, your new consciousness picks out the book you want when you want it. But you believe your old, transplanted consciousness as a moving ribbon, a playback of your old life where you have no choice over the sequence of events. And, you say, you are actually re-living these events, not just witnessing them.

AUTHOR: Now, can I indulge in a little personal fantasy?

KIERKEGAARD: Your whole hypothesis is a big personal fantasy.

AUTHOR: I know, but this is more imaginative still.

KIERKEGAARD: Will I find it entertaining?

AUTHOR: Yes. The universe is in flux. There's nothing permanent in it. Things are continually being created and destroyed. But—here's my point! there is a permanent record of everything that has been experienced by all thinking beings trans-located to subatomic space. Nothing has been lost. The universe is temporary, but our experience of it is permanent. Permanently recorded in subatomic space. God's record of his handiwork, if you like.

KIERKEGAARD: Your intuition is very agile.

AUTHOR: Intuition is often wrong.

KIERKEGAARD: Usually wrong.

AUTHOR: Have it your way.

KIERKEGAARD: Will you join me for lunch?

AUTHOR: Thought you'd never ask. I've been wondering where you keep your appetite.

Both men become less serious. An order is given to the waitress who soon returns with ham rashers, bacon, poached eggs, hashed brown spuds, buttered rolls, and steaming coffee. The two philosophers leisurely scoff up these victuals and, comfortably full, resume their intense dialogue between sips of coffee.

KIERKEGAARD: I have a few more questions. Just a few.

AUTHOR: Be my guest.

KIERKEGAARD: I don't want to bore you.

AUTHOR: No, no.

KIERKEGAARD: Well, here's my first. Many people have a strong faith in God. What are they to think about your ideas of life after death?

AUTHOR: Well, that's up to them. I see no conflict. My book doesn't oppose faith in a god. It is simply silent on the subject. The

Saved Consciousness Hypothesis tries to extrapolate from observed facts. Religion is mostly anecdote.

KIERKEGAARD: The true believer does not need facts. His or her belief is founded in what I call a leap of faith. I have observed this in many, many people. It has been a study of mine. People are not really interested in facts when it comes to God.

AUTHOR: Nevertheless, I try to point to facts, wherever I can find them.

KIERKEGAARD: Do you believe in God?

AUTHOR: May I quote you, Kierkegaard, in this matter? He wrote, "Where is the manager? I would like to see him." In other words, Kierkegaard looked for a manager, but could find no evidence of one. Personally, I believe that the works of nature are the only evidence we have of a manager.

KIERKEGAARD: Perhaps this world and the works of nature are just an illusion fabricated by our minds.

AUTHOR: No, I don't believe that. This world gives us a powerful platform from which to study our existence. We are not just pushing on a string that falls away. We have tangible things to manipulate that react to our push.

KIERKEGAARD: Maybe we are just manipulating these things in our imagination.

AUTHOR: Doesn't matter, we are still manipulating them. If I sip this coffee, it makes no difference to me whether I'm imagining it or not. As far as I'm concerned, it tastes good.

KIERKEGAARD: Why did you write this book?

AUTHOR: It sort of wrote itself. If there's a door to pass through, some of us would like to know what's on the other side. I'm simply offering suggestions.

KIERKEGAARD: What do you think is on the other side?

AUTHOR: Perhaps you, Kierkegaard, would not mind telling me?

KIERKEGAARD: I'm not at liberty.

AUTHOR: Consciousness continues to exist on the other side, but our body and brain don't. You are already familiar with the mechanism I propose.

KIERKEGAARD: May I ask you again, do you believe in God?

AUTHOR: Which God? Christian, Jewish, Muslim, Hindu? They are all quite different, as you must know. You are s student of theology.

KIERKEGAARD: Take your choice. Any God?

AUTHOR: My logic tells me that the Universe must have a source.

KIERKEGAARD: Your logic, not faith. Why not faith?

AUTHOR: I was born with a brain. I try to use it.

KIERKEGAARD: Man's brain is limited. Can you tell me why people, even those with faith, fear death?

AUTHOR: It is instinctive, a healthy instinct. If we didn't fear death, we would all be dead.

KIERKEGAARD: How credible do you think your hypothesis is? You will agree that there is nothing in your Saved Consciousness Hypothesis that has been proven to be true?

AUTHOR: Absolutely, I agree. That's why it's called a hypothesis.

KIERKEGAARD: Do you think that there is any way your Hypothesis could be tested and proven either to be true or false?

AUTHOR: Sure. This is a job for physicists and neuroscientists. The Hypothesis deals with electric voltages, and these can be measured. We know we can measure electric voltages in nerves. The question is, can we find the electric voltages in the brain that form consciousness and map their route? Can we find the final common pathway? I hope this search will be done in humans rather than experimental animals. Humans shouldn't object. There are no pain receptors in the brain, and humans can tell us what they are thinking.

KIERKEGAARD: Is there actually work being done on this?

AUTHOR: There is. Various labs are working on consciousness. For example, Crick and Koch in California have traced some visual pathways in the brain and related them to consciousness. There are different ways of identifying neural pathways. You can use voltage probes that are direct and specific. They're the best. You can use indirect methods such as fMRI and PET. The electron microscope and radioautographs are also useful. The trick is to find if and how all the neural pathways converge to form a final common pathway of consciousness, if they do.

KIERKEGAARD: Why choose the subatomic world for the storage of your consciousness wave?

AUTHOR: Haven't we covered that? It has multiple dimensions. Anything can happen there by what is called the superposition of waves. The subatomic world occupies the same space as the nerve networks where consciousness and memory exist. They touch.

KIERKEGAARD: I have a slightly bizarre question for you. Does the cult of spiritualism fit into your hypothesis? There have been well known people that have believed in spiritualism.

AUTHOR: Oh, I know about that. You mean talking to the dead?

KIERKEGAARD: Yes. Communicating with the dead.

AUTHOR: According to you, I'm talking to the dead right now. Yourself.

KIERKEGAARD: Please, let's not get into that. I am referring to people who think they can communicate with the dead through a gifted "medium."

AUTHOR: No, no, no. My hypothesis has nothing to do with spiritualism. But I'm surprised at the number of famous and able people that have believed in what seems to me to be a lot of malarkey. For instance, take well-known writers like Conan Doyle, Lewis Carol, Alfred Tennyson, Mark Twain. They are supposed to have believed it. Also politicians with high profiles; prime ministers such as William Gladstone and Mackenzie King. And how about recognized scientists like physicist Sir Oliver Lodge, and naturalist Alfred Wallace. All capable people in their fields. But believers in hocus-pocus.

KIERKEGAARD: You sound very skeptical. Why shouldn't they believe?

AUTHOR: Well, believe what you want. But it's been made clear that the "mediums" associated with spiritualism have mostly been actors, crooks, or psychotics with multiple personalities. Houdini called them vultures. He said that any good magician could pull off the same stunt in a darkened room. These believers in spiritualism shut their eyes to contrary evidence. They want to believe. They don't expect fraud. There's a good account of this in Rawcliffe's book which he calls *Occult and Supernatural Phenomena* [1].

KIERKEGAARD: Published by Baywood?

AUTHOR: No, Dover.

KIERKEGAARD: Changing the subject once more, I have a question about life, not death. Do you think alien civilizations exist in the universe, and if so, why haven't we heard from them? Do you have views on that?

AUTHOR: Well, most star systems we see are very far away and quite young. When their light set out for us, they were too young to have formed advanced intelligence. That takes a lot of time. There would presumably be no beings created in that short span of time capable of signaling us. On the other hand, the nearer stars that we see, like those in the Milky Way, are older and have had time to develop intelligent beings. But should we expect their signals? I don't know. Could they locate the Earth, which would be dark to them? Where would they get the power to signal us? Serious astronomers are looking. There's a lot in the literature under SETI, meaning search for extraterrestrial intelligence. So far, no results except radio noise [2].

KIERKEGAARD: I don't want to exceed my welcome, but may I ask you a little bit about your personal philosophy on human existence. I know I've already taken up a lot of your time, and you have been very generous.

AUTHOR: You want more of my guesswork?

KIERKEGAARD: I find your guesswork interesting. My question is, why are we here? How can we best use our time on Earth except just to survive like a leaf on a tree?

AUTHOR: Well, there are two things that I can think of. First, to relieve suffering, and second, to understand the Universe. This is intuitive bias with nothing to back it up scientifically. Touchy-feely stuff, some would call it.

KIERKEGAARD: What about happiness?

AUTHOR: That comes with the first two.

KIERKEGAARD: If there is a God, why does God allow suffering?

AUTHOR: I tend to think of it this way. If suffering is part of creation, maybe it's an unwanted side effect. This is all very sloppy thinking, what?

KIERKEGAARD: You have said that you are not qualified to talk about purpose.

AUTHOR: Do you see any evidence of purpose in the universe? The universe is running down, but intelligence is running up. Is that purpose? Perhaps the universe is only a spin-off of some larger creation that has purpose, but we're not smart enough to see it. We'll have to up-grade our intelligence first.

KIERKEGAARD: I agree with you. Man is very limited in what he can know.

AUTHOR: Well, we're not very smart at the moment, but that doesn't speak for the future. Given time, we'll break through all the present knowledge barriers. If we live long enough.

KIERKEGAARD: Yes, but in the meantime we will suffer.

AUTHOR: No question about that.

KIERKEGAARD: Another thought comes to me. Have you noticed that the universe seems to have a lot of unnecessary hardware? What does God want with all those galaxies and energy? Whatever his purpose might be, does he need all that equipment to achieve it?

AUTHOR: You know the value of redundancy. A fish may lay a thousand eggs for one to survive. The surplus of energy and equipment in the universe makes the evolution of intelligence assured. Any alleged God that might want to create intelligence would need that redundancy. That's my reasoning. If one region is annihilated by a collision, an explosion, or a black hole, there are plenty of other regions where intelligence can take root. Astronomers tell me that our own galaxy is due for a collision with Andromeda in about three billion years. Then there's always the question of parallel universes to add to the redundancy. They might provide for the evolution of different kinds of intelligence, making a more interesting mix. Without redundancy, it seems to me doubtful that intelligence would emerge in creation.

KIERKEGAARD: Do you think that human intelligence will evolve further?

AUTHOR: Yes, definitely. Unless we do something foolish like self-destruct. That's a real danger.

KIERKEGAARD: Can we prevent self-destruction?

AUTHOR: The population explosion, it seems to me, makes it likely that we will self-destruct unless we can control it. Population pressure could lead to nuclear war, anarchy, plague, pestilence, all that sort of thing. Too many people, not enough space. This could put us back to the stone age. Simple survival would be the order of the day. Don't you think we've got a time bomb here?

KIERKEGAARD: You sound like Malthus.

AUTHOR: No, not really. In his time, there were merely millions of people, not billions. Now we have billions. I can almost hear Carl Sagan, "and soon there will be billions upon billions upon billions!"

KIERKEGAARD: Could we escape this crowding by going underground, or perhaps leave the planet?

AUTHOR: I don't think so. I think, instead, we will succeed in stopping our numbers from multiplying beyond our means to sustain them. Or nature will do the job for us.

KIERKEGAARD: One supposes that the struggle for survival is the reason that intelligence has got to where it is today. Competition puts selection pressure on the brain.

Kierkegaard takes a breath, empties his tankard, and sucks up the remaining froth through pursed lips.

KIERKEGAARD: Now, may I change the subject once more?

AUTHOR: You're putting a lot of pressure on my brain.

KIERKEGAARD: The last point on which I would like to have your views is what is called determinism. Some say that when your time comes, you will die. Nothing can stop it. Nothing you or anyone else can do. Your death has been predetermined.

AUTHOR: That is classical theory. It says that everything in the universe is predetermined. In other words, if you know the position, mass, velocity, charge, spin, and so forth, of every particle in the universe at any one time, then you can predict exactly what the universe will be like at any other time. Simple cause and effect.

KIERKEGAARD: Do you agree with this?

AUTHOR: Well, according to Heisenberg's uncertainty principle, you cannot know all these things about even one particle at any one time, let alone all the particles in the universe. That would seem to put a big limit on prediction.

KIERKEGAARD: Then how could a creator of the universe predict the emergence of intelligence? How could it be planned in advance when events are unpredictable? How could God bring this off?

AUTHOR: Perhaps the creator doesn't buy Heisenberg.

KIERKEGAARD: Yes, but can you start out with a ball of hydrogen gas and predict that it will turn into humans?

AUTHOR: Well, the creator did. Or did he?

KIERKEGAARD: What do you think is the potential for the human brain?

AUTHOR: Interesting question. I personally think the potential for the human brain has to do with expanding its computing power. Increasing its intelligence by human intervention. Intelligence, it seems to me, is all about insight. A monkey gets a banana by reaching through the bars of its cage with a stick. Using the stick requires insight. Something clicks in the brain of the monkey and it suddenly sees how to get the banana. Quick as lightning. That's insight. It happens in a flash.

KIERKEGAARD: And how does one expand the brain's capacity for insight?

AUTHOR: That's the big question. I see many possibilities. It's possible for humans to increase their brain power by various ways. One is through genetic engineering. By that I mean gene manipulation. But we're looking way, way down the road for that. In the nearer term, one could invent electronic attachments. People are working on that. I'm talking about an actual interface between brain and computer, perhaps using electrodes. A sophisticated microprocessor, harnessed to the brain, would give you a scary amount of power. Your thinking could consist of wall-to-wall insights. Concepts you can simultaneously store and inter-relate in your brain in an instant of time.

KIERKEGAARD: Ah! Insights again.

AUTHOR: You must consider what's happening with computers. You know about Moore's doubling law, and new gadgets like bio-molecular switches. We've only seen the tip of the iceberg. Let's call the computer-assisted brain a thinking system. If you could link these thinking-systems up to one another, you would get the benefit of synergism. Each one assisting the other so that the whole was greater than the parts. Hey, we could even connect up to alien brains, if they exist.

KIERKEGAARD: Are you, perhaps, extrapolating too far?

AUTHOR: Do you think so? I could take it even farther. The whole network might even interface with God, the sort of thing that the Eastern religions talk about. A merging of the soul with God.

KIERKEGAARD: A God whose existence many do not acknowledge. Now Sir, I must go and not take up any more of your time.

* * *

The stranger calling himself Kierkegaard rises from the table (a little wobbly, mind you) and goes to the washroom for the fifth time. On returning, he thanks the Author for the hospitality accorded him, and says he hopes they will meet again. The Author shakes the stranger's hand, escorts him to the tavern door, and watches as he navigates a convoluted course down the street.

Sitting down once more, the Author stares into the middle distance. He wonders about this man calling himself Kierkegaard, about their unexpected talk, about his, the Author's, own fanciful musings. He reflects on his Hypothesis concerning life after death, and orders another draft ale to assist his thinking. Did the stranger believe the Hypothesis of Saved Consciousness to be credible? The Author doesn't know. He had forgotten to ask. And he hadn't autographed the stranger's book. Bad oversight. Too much beer, no doubt. He decides that today will be the day to do something about his beer consumption. He will restrict it. No, he will go cold turkey. That's the way, cold turkey!

The Author pushes his brimming tankard away and pays the waitress. He goes to the door and, without a backward glance, resolutely leaves this favorite watering hole. Future thirsts, he decides, will be slaked at the tea-and-muffin shop around the corner. He will inform Janis at the Publisher's office about the tea-and-muffin shop in case the stranger calling himself Kierkegaard wants to come and talk again. The Author would like that.

REFERENCES

1. D. H. Rawcliffe, *Occult and Supernatural Phenomena,* Dover, New York, 1959.
2. G. Gonzalez and P. Ward, Refuges for Life in a Hostile Universe, *Scientific American,* pp. 60-67, October 2001.

APPENDIX I

Recycled Life Versus New Life

The Saved Conscious Hypothesis has only to do with a recycled life. It predicts a re-run of the present life, the life we are living now. We take our present life with us, the good parts and the bad. The voltage numbers of our past consciousness are constantly being recorded in subatomic space, available for regeneration after death. This is referred to as recycling.

This is quite different to the idea of a new life. A new life, by definition, is not a recycled one. A new life suggests new experiences, not just a repeat of the old. By a new life is meant a vastly different life that may (or may not) await us after death. The Saved Consciousness Hypothesis is mostly silent on the subject of a new life. It talks mainly about recycling past experiences.

There is presently no physical evidence for a new life, no obvious directions for research. Opinions regarding a new life after death are to be found in the scriptures, and also in the literature concerning "metaphysics." The Saved Consciousness Hypothesis has little to say on the subject of new post-mortem lives except to allow for the possibility of superposed lives as part of an individual's "wave function." This means that different forks in the road of consciousness could be precipitated from the consciousness wave that might lead to altered lives. This was discussed in chapter 2 under the heading *Speculations.*

APPENDIX II

Making Protein

Watson and Crick opened the window through which it is possible to observe the incredible achievement of the cell in organizing the gala dance of amino acids as they lock arms to form the proteins of life. The basic maneuvers of the dance are mechanical and straightforward. That is what Arthur Murray taught in his one, two, three-step diagrams. Get from A to B in the right order, don't trip up, and always follow instructions. The Arthur Murray motto is also the plan of action followed by amino acid molecules as they construct proteins. Let's see if we can trace some of their dance steps.

Our first step in following the cha-cha-cha that constructs proteins is to recognize how the dancing instructions are printed on the DNA molecule so that they may be conveyed to the amino acid molecules waiting in the wings. The DNA molecule, you may remember, is composed of two very long threads, each containing nucleotide units A, T, C, and G attached in series like links in a chain. Now, here comes a critical point in our story: each of the twenty amino acids in the cell recognizes one particular sequence of three nucleotides, called a codon. When an amino acid sees these special nucleotides in a row, it is permitted to shout: "Hey, that codon is for me, and only for me!" Unfortunately for the simplicity of our account, another issue must be introduced. The amino acids are in the cytoplasm outside the nucleus and so do not have direct contact with DNA which is contained within the nucleus in the nucleoplasm. How, then, can the amino acids outside find out about the nucleotide sequences on the DNA molecules inside? DNA itself provides the solution to this problem. It sends a messenger out of the nucleus among the amino acids, and this messenger carries the same pattern of nucleotide sequences that are inscribed on the DNA. This messenger molecule is called messenger RNA, or m-RNA for short.

The nucleotide sequence for one single protein takes up only a short segment of a DNA chain. Let's imagine a protein that is made up of a string of one hundred amino acids. Since each amino acid recognizes a special sequence of three nucleotides, in order to make the protein we would need a DNA strand of three hundred nucleotides in correct sequence to carry the code for our protein. What happens is this: DNA unwinds its two strands to lay bare the three hundred nucleotides, then copies that sequence in the form of an m-RNA messenger molecule. This m-RNA copy leaves the nucleus to find the amino acids in the cytoplasm outside the nucleus.

Now, further complications. We would like to introduce you to another cell organelle called the ribosome. These small, dense bodies populate the cell cytoplasm in numbers almost too large to count. What do these organelles do to earn their keep? They are central to our amino acid dance, for it is on ribosomes that protein molecules are constructed from amino acids. Also, it is to the ribosomes that m-RNA messenger molecules, with their special nucleotide sequences, become attached after they leave the nucleus.

Let's summarize:

1. DNA in the nucleus carries the code for constructing all of the proteins made in the cell;
2. DNA duplicates this code in short segments called m-RNA molecules;
3. m-RNA molecules leave the nucleus and attach themselves to the ribosome organelles in the cytoplasm of the cell.

What happens now? Where do we go next in the dance of the amino acids? We will focus our attention on a final complication to our story. This complication takes the form of a molecule called transfer RNA, or t-RNA. These t-RNA molecules, swimming freely in the cytoplasm with the amino acids, can be thought of as having two ends: one end wants to hold hands with one particular kind of amino acid, whereas the other end is only interested in linking up with a particular codon, or nucleotide sequence, on the m-RNA molecule. These attachments do, indeed, occur. First, the t-RNA finds and attaches to its favorite amino acid with one end, then the t-RNA/amino acid combination locks by its other end to its matching codon on the m-RNA thread. The ribosome (remember it?) acts as a policeman directing traffic, seeing to it that the t-RNA/amino acid groups are added in line, one at a time like letters to a word, along the length of the m-RNA thread. As the t-RNA/amino acid groups are lined up in this fashion, each amino acid grabs its neighbor's hand in a daisy chain. The chain, on reaching the right length with the correct number of amino acid molecules, is released from the m-RNA thread as a bona fide protein. This ingenious amino acid dance, with all its intricate steps, continues unabated throughout the life of the cell. The music stops when cell death occurs, bringing a halt to the antics of the whirling dancers.

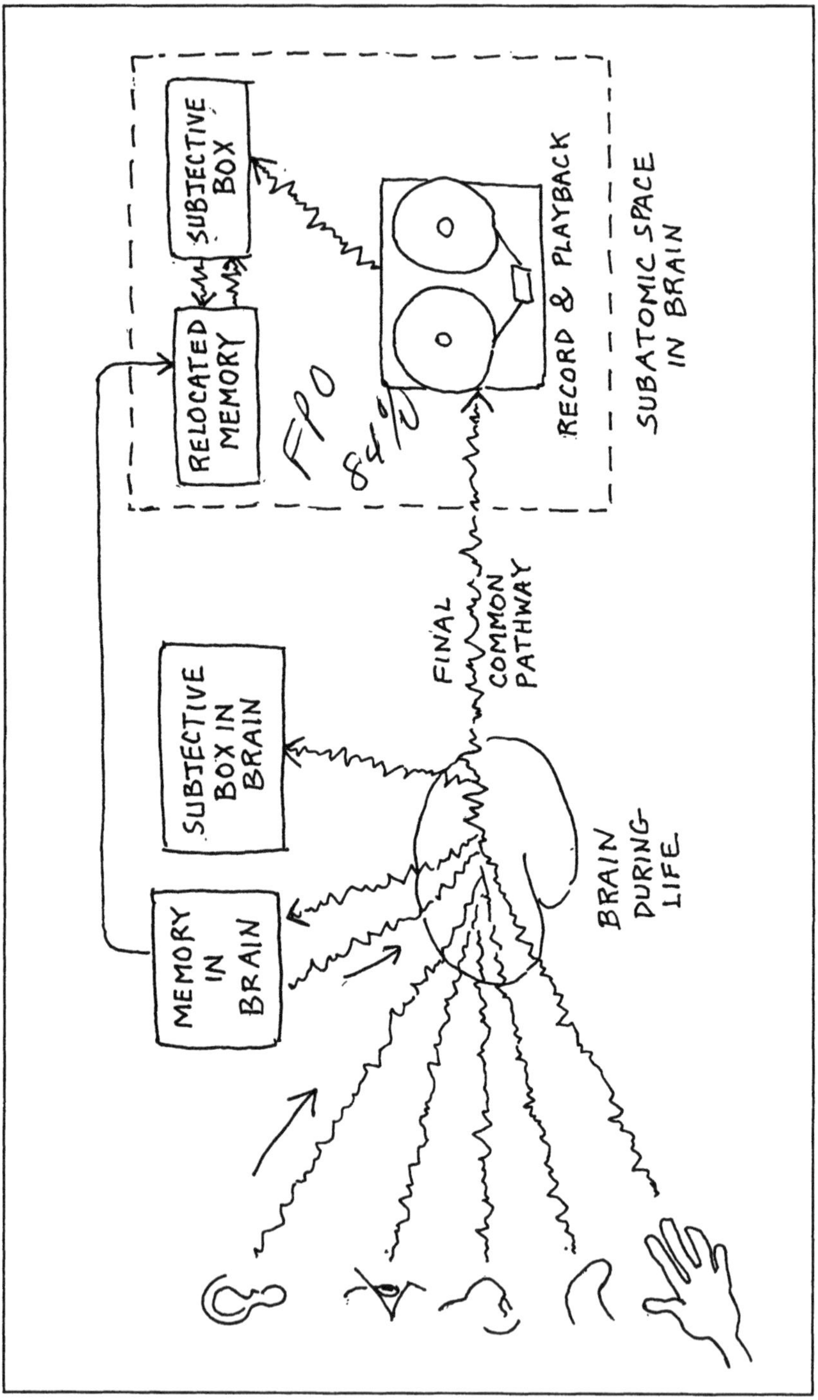
MEMORY IN BRAIN
SUBJECTIVE BOX IN BRAIN
BRAIN DURING LIFE
FINAL COMMON PATHWAY
RELOCATED MEMORY
SUBJECTIVE BOX
FPO
84%
RECORD & PLAYBACK
SUBATOMIC SPACE IN BRAIN

Figure 1.

APPENDIX III

The Saved Consciousness Hypothesis

(See Figure 1, p. 152)

1. The components of consciousness start with the sense receptors. These provide voltage impulses in nerve fibers going to the brain. These voltage impulses are the raw materials of consciousness.

2. The output from the senses converges through a series of processing regions to a Final Common Pathway. This may consist of synchronized neuronal impulses resonating in many parts of the brain.

3. The Final Common Pathway has outputs to, and inputs from, the memory. The memory itself is a nerve network that preserves a record of voltage impulses sent to it by the Final Common Pathway.

4. The main output of the Final Common Pathway is a composite wave of the senses and memory referred to as the Objective Consciousness wave. It may be superposed on a carrier wave. This main output goes to two principal destinations.

5. One output of these destinations is the Subjective Consciousness Box (nerve network) in the brain which processes the wave to produce subjective consciousness.

6. The second output of the Objective Consciousness wave goes to adjacent subatomic space where it is recorded.

7. The recorded Objective Consciousness wave in the subatomic quantum field has the potential of being replayed. The output goes to a subjective box in subatomic space converting the wave to subjective consciousness.

APPENDIX IV

Random Assortment & Crossover

Although *new* traits arise spontaneously in a species by mutation, *existing* traits are passed from parents to offspring in new combinations that do not involve mutation. The diverse parental traits form a mix in the fertilized egg that produces an individual different from either parent. Thus, Mary may get her Mom's blue eyes and blond hair, but inherit her Dad's long legs and freckles. The mix is brought about by processes known as random assortment and crossover of chromosomes.

1. In fertilized eggs, chromosomes (and therefore genes) come in pairs, one from the father and one from the mother. Each member, or allele, of the pair is different in the effect it can produce which, as Mendel noted, may be "dominant" or "recessive" in character. A dominant "allele" (D), for example, might produce a trait such as the production of pigment, whereas its recessive allele (d) might produce none. If the allele combination in the fertilized cell should be (DD) or (Dd), pigment would be produced; if (dd), it would not. There are many germ cells, each carrying one of these alleles, which could combine at fertilization. Which alleles actually do end up together as a pair in the fertilized cell is a chance event, and hence the process is referred to as "random assortment" of genes.
2. The randomness of allele recombination in the fertilized egg is increased by another process called "crossover." This occurs in the parent germ cell during meiotic division when paired chromosomes lie side by side and exchange segments of DNA and the genes which are located on those segments. It is as if ten red-coated soldiers forming part of a long line were to change places with ten blue-coated soldiers opposite them in another long line. When these chromosomes separate at cell division, they will contain interchanged segments, thus increasing their diversity.

The overall result of random assortment and crossover of chromosomes is to provide a greater variety of trait combinations in an organism's offspring, and hence improve the species' chances of successfully meeting new challenges in a changing environment. Johnny might succumb, but his brother Jim, endowed with a more suitable combination of traits, might flourish and breed.

APPENDIX V

Cell Energy

The form of energy that is used best by animal cells comes from a molecule known as ATP which is made in the cell by a process, as has already been noted, called oxidative phosphorylation. In this process the food, let's say glucose sugar, is dismantled chemically in the cell, and this dismantling causes the sugar to lose some energy which, it turns out, the cell cannot use directly for its work. However, the cell is able instead to take the energy released by the sugar and use it to upgrade a relatively low energy molecule called ADP into the higher energy molecule ATP. The cell can draw upon this energy reserve at will for its many needs by breaking down ATP again to ADP. The reaction is reversible. This conversion back and forth between ATP and ADP with the transfer and release of energy is going on continually inside the cell. The released energy is used by the cell to power the incredible number and variety of chemical reactions involved in its daily work. The cell may not have a brain, but its manipulations, such as obtaining energy from sugar, proceed flawlessly, are self directed, and go on twenty-four hours a day.

The conversion of ADP to ATP by phosphorylation occurs in the interior of cell organelles called mitochondria, and requires oxygen that is obtained by diffusion into the cell. The phosphorylation reaction also requires the participation of fifty or more enzymes, made from protein, which must be positioned relative to one another in a very exact spatial sequence for the reaction to occur. Evidence shows that these enzymes are lined up in the appropriate order within and upon infoldings of the mitochondrial membrane. It is here that the high energy ATP molecules are formed, and from here that they travel out of the mitochondrion to reach the rest of the cell.

APPENDIX VI

Tweaking the Consciousness Wave

Suppose we could fiddle with the consciousness wave. By this, I mean change its form, alter its shape. What if we could manipulate the wave to our liking? The wave is, after all, postulated to be mere voltage numbers, and voltage numbers can be changed. We change them, for example, when we take an aspirin, narcotic, or anesthetic for pain. By so doing, we have changed the voltages that gave us our consciousness of pain.

Suppose, instead of taking an aspirin, we do the job more directly. Suppose we could manipulate the consciousness wave to remove or reduce the pain components by electronically tweaking it. Put away the aspirin bottle and, instead, feed the wave through an hypothetical microchip to alter the pain inflections by inputting new voltages. By direct electronic input, we alter any part of the wave we choose, whether it is to remove pain or for some other desired purpose. A highly speculative, but perhaps a reasonably logical concept. The idea could apply to changing the shape of the consciousness wave in real life with its practical applications. It could apply equally well to changing the consciousness wave, if such exists, after death.

Back to music again. I would like to give you a real example of making changes to a voltage wave. I have a friend by the name of Gerry who is a recording engineer and musician. Gerry spends much of his time sitting at a computer tweaking voltage waves. In this case, the voltage wave represents music that Gerry has recorded, let's say the sound of his clarinet. If a certain note is not right, not in tune for example, he can change it so it will be in tune. He does this by tweaking the voltage wave.

Keep in mind here, please, that we will compare what Gerry does to his musical note in the studio with what might be done to some life event on the consciousness wave in the brain, or on the wave after it has been hypothetically recorded in space. This would require appropriate software interfacing with the consciousness wave.

In Gerry's case, the software is Mark of the Unicorn Digital Performer v 2.6, together with Digidesign Sound Designer II. He uses this software to alter his clarinet note in various ways. He can eliminate the note, shorten or lengthen it, raise or lower it, make it come in sooner or later, create a crescendo or decrescendo, modify the attack, or change the timbre. He can fiddle with the note as he likes by typing in the right voltage changes to give him the desired result.

If changes can be made to one voltage wave, they can be made to another. Theoretically, changes can be made to the consciousness voltage wave, assuming such a thing exists. If there is a consciousness wave as I have postulated, then the potential is there to alter it and thereby improve things from the human standpoint. If it were possible to identify the wave forms of pain, or of hallucinations, delusions, obsessive compulsions, and so on, these could be eliminated or modified by punching in the right voltages. In life, the punching in might be done by a suitably programmed chip implanted in the brain. At present, we can only speculate on the possibility of such technology.

If we now talk about modifying the recorded consciousness voltage wave in space after death, the same ideas apply, only in this case the wave might be modified to change any part of the life we have subjectively experienced. You may remember that the Saved Consciousness Hypothesis postulates the entire wave of our conscious life is saved in subatomic space and may be regenerated after death. According to this Appendix, the potential exists to change or edit this post mortem consciousness. The wave could be tweaked to remove or alter any component. Pain or distress might simply be filtered out of our recycled life. Perhaps Nature has the sophisticated programmable software to do this.

What about the provision of new conscious experience after death? What about a new conscious life after death rather than just recycling the old?

Any wave has the potential to exist in an infinite number of forms. If there is indeed the preservation of a consciousness wave after death, then one can speculate that it could be modified to take an infinite number of new shapes. In this way, new conscious experiences have the potential to be introduced after death. Possibly Nature re-shapes the recorded consciousness wave by inputting new voltages. This might explain how consciousness after death could consist of something other than the recycling of the old consciousness wave, and make the idea of death more palatable by opening up the prospect of new experience.

Additional Readings

Adams, C. J., Islam, *The World Book Encyclopedia,* Chicago, 1983.

Angus, Samuel, *The Mystery-Religions and Christianity,* Carol, New York, 1966.

Asimov, Isaac, *Understanding Physics,* Mentor, New York, 1969.

Asimov, Issac, *Asimov's Guide to the Bible,* Wings Books, New Jersey, 1968-69.

Asphaug, Erik, The Small Planets, *Scientific American,* May 2000.

Auer Falk, N. E., Mysticism, *The World Book Encyclopedia,* Chicago, 1983.

Baggott, Jim, *The Meaning of Quantum Theory,* Oxford University Press, New York, 1992.

Beardsley, T., NASA Wants to Fend Off Doomsday Asteroids, *Scientific American,* November 1991.

Beck, Sara C., Dwarf Galaxies & Starbursts, *Scientific American,* June 2000.

Blake, N. M., Bryan, *The World Book Encyclopedia,* Chicago, 1983.

Bossomaier, T. and D. Green, *Patterns in the Sand,* Helix Books, Massachusetts, 1998.

Brown, J. H., Evolution, *The World Book Encyclopedia,* Chicago, 1983.

Bucher, Martin A. and David Spergel, Inflation in a Low-Density Universe, *Scientific American,* January 1999.

Calder, Nigel, *Einstein's Universe,* Viking Penguin, New York, 1979.

Caldwell, Robert R. and Marc Kamionkawski, Echoes from the Big Bang, *Scientific American,* January 2001.

Capecchi, Mario R., Targeted Gene Replacement, *Scientific American,* March 1994.

Capps, W. H., Religion, *World Book Encyclopedia,* Chicago, 1983.

Chiao, R. Y., P. G. Kwiat, A. M. Steinberg, Faster Than Light? *Scientific American,* August 1993.

Crawford, Ian, Where are They? *Scientific American,* July 2000.

Damasio, Antonio R., How the Brain Creates the Mind, *Scientific American,* December 1999.

Dawkins, Richard, God's Utility Function, *Scientific American,* November 1995.

Doolittle, W. Ford, Uprooting the Tree of Life, *Scientific American,* February 2000.

Doyle, L. R., H-J. Deeg, and T. M. Brown, Searching for Shadows of Other Earths, *Scientific American,* September 2000.

Ellison, Jr., S. P., Earth, *The World Book Encyclopedia,* Chicago, 1983.

Feynman, Richard, *QED,* Princeton University Press, New Jersey, 1988.
Finch, C. E. and L. Hayflick, *The Biology of Aging,* Van Nostrand Reinhold, New York, 1977.
Frankel, E., *DNA: The Ladder of Life,* McGraw-Hill, New York, 1979.
Franklin, Stan, *Artificial Minds,* MIT Press, Massachusetts, 1995.
Freedman, W. L., The Expansion Rate and Size of the Universe, *Scientific American,* November 1992.
Gehrels, Tom, Collisions with Comets and Asteroids, *Scientific American,* March 1996.
Goldman-Rakik, Working Memory and the Mind, *Scientific American,* September 1992.
Gregor Johann, D. L. Hartl Muslims, and C. J. Adams, Mendel, *The World Book Encyclopedia,* Chicago, 1983.
Harpur, Tom, *Life After Death,* McClelland & Stewart, Toronto, 1992.
Hawking, Stephen, *Black Holes and Baby Universes,* Bantam, New York, 1993.
Hartl, D. L. Heredity, *The World Book Encyclopedia,* Chicago, 1983.
Hartl, D. L., Mutation, *The World Book Encyclopedia,* Chicago, 1983.
Hinton, G. E., How Neural Networks Learn from Experience, *Scientific American,* September 1992.
Holland, John H., *Emergence,* Helix Books, Massachusetts, 1998.
Horgan, John, Can Science Explain Consciousness? *Scientific American,* July 1994.
Horgan, John, Measuring Eternity, *Scientific American,* December 1990.
Horgan, John, Particle Metaphysics, *Scientific American,* February 1994.
Horgan, John, Profile: Edward Witten, *Scientific American,* November 1991.
Horgan, John, Profile: Karl R. Popper, *Scientific American,* November 1992.
Horgan, John, The World According to RNA, *Scientific American,* January 1996.
Jick, L. A., Jews, *The World Book Encyclopedia,* Chicago, 1983.
Johnson, R. F., Bible, *The World Book Encyclopedia,* Chicago, 1983.
Kafatos, M. and R. Nadeau, *The Conscious Universe,* Springer-Verlag, New York, 1990.
Kauffman, Stuart, *At Home in the Universe,* Oxford University Press, New York, 1995.
Kirshner, Robert P., The Earth's Elements, *Scientific American,* October 1994.
Krauss, L. M. And G. D. Starkman, The Fate of Life in the Universe, *Scientific American,* November 1999.
Leakey, Richard, Extinction Past and Present, *Time,* Special Edition, Spring 2000.
Lemonick, M. and A. Dorfman, Up from the Apes, *Time Magazine,* August 23, 1999.
LePage, A. J., Where They Could Hide, *Scientific American,* July 2000.
Littleton, C. S., Mythology, *The World Book Encyclopedia,* Chicago, 1983.
Logothetis, N. K., Vision: A Window on Consciousness, *Scientific American,* November 1999.
Lusted, Hugh S., Controlling Computers with Neural Signals, *Scientific American,* October 1996.
Malhotra, Renu, Migrating Planets, *Scientific American,* September 1999.

Martindale, D., More Than A Wobble, *Scientific American,* p. 27, February 2000.
May, R. M., How Many Species Inhabit the Earth, *Scientific American,* October 1992.
Miller, P. M., The Wind and Donald O. Hebb, *Scientific American,* January 1993.
Moravec, Hans, Rise of the Robots, *Scientific American,* December 1999.
Morgan, John, Off to an Early Start, *Scientific American,* August 1993.
Mukerjee, Madhusree, Explaining Everything, *Scientific American,* January 1996.
Nauen, Stroud, Yeazell, The Classical Limit of an Atom, *Scientific American,* June 1994.
Neusner, Jacob, Judaism, *The World Book Encyclopedia,* Chicago, 1983.
Penrose, Roger, *The Emperor's New Mind,* Penguin, Oxford University Press, New York, 1989.
Penrose, Roger, *Shadows of the Mind,* Penguin, Oxford University Press, New York, 1989.
Pond, C. M., Darwin, Charles Robert, *The World Book Encyclopedia,* Chicago, 1983.
Powell, Corey S. Star Gobbler, *Scientific American,* August 1994.
Ranson, S. W. and S. L. Clark, *The Anatomy of the Nervous System,* Saunders, Pennsylvania, 1951.
Rees, Martin, Exploring our Universe and Others, *Scientific American,* December 1999.
Reynolds, F. E., Buddhism, *The World Book Encyclopedia,* Chicago, 1983.
Rigby, P. W. J., Genetics, *The World Book Encyclopedia,* Chicago, 1983.
Roger, J. and Neville Woolf, Searching for Life on Other Planets, *Scientific American,* April 1996.
Rose, Michael R., Can Human Aging be Postponed? *Scientific American,* December 1999.
Ross, N.W., *Buddhism,* Vintage Books, New York, 1981.
Rothman, Tony, *Instant Physics,* Byron Press, New York, 1995.
Rubenstein, Irwin, Cell, *The World Book Encyclopedia,* Chicago, 1983.
Sagan, Carl, The Search for Extraterrestrial Life, *Scientific American,* October 1994.
Schrodinger, Erwin, *What is Life?* Cambridge University Press, United Kingdom, 1958.
Sharp, L. W., *Fundamentals of Cytology,* McGraw-Hill, New York, 1943.
Skatz, C. J., The Developing Brain, *Scientific American,* September 1992.
Stix, Gary, Getting More from Moore's, *Scientific American,* April 2001.
Stix, Gary, Waiting for Breakthroughs, *Scientific American,* April 1996.
Swenson, G. W., Jr., Intragalactically Speaking, *Scientific American,* July 2000.
Tarter, Jill C. and C. Chyba, Is there Life Elsewhere in the Universe? *Scientific American,* pp. 118-123, December 1999.
Tattersall, Ian, Once We Were Not Alone, *Scientific American,* January 2000.
Tipler, Frank J., *The Physics of Immortality,* Doubleday, New York, 1994.
Trinh Xuan Thuan, *The Secret Melody,* Oxford University Press, New York, 1995.
Weindruch, Richard, Caloric Restriction and Aging, *Scientific American,* January 1996.

Weinberg, Steven, A Unified Physics by 2050, *Scientific American,* December 1999.
Weinberg, Steven, Life in the Universe, *Scientific American,* October 1994.
White, C. S. J., Hinduism, *The World Book Encyclopedia,* Chicago, 1983.
White, Chandler Smith, *Principles of Biochemistry,* McGraw-Hill, New York, 1959.
Yam, Philip, Life from Scratch, *Scientific American,* February 2000.
Yam, Philip, Mr. Spock, Phone Home, *Scientific American,* October 2000.
York, Derek, The Earliest History of the Earth, *Scientific American,* January 1993.

Index

For Product Safety Concerns and Information please contact our EU
representative GPSR@taylorandfrancis.com
Taylor & Francis Verlag GmbH, Kaufingerstraße 24, 80331 München, Germany

www.ingramcontent.com/pod-product-compliance
Ingram Content Group UK Ltd.
Pitfield, Milton Keynes, MK11 3LW, UK
UKHW022120190926
475702UK00013B/1559

* 9 7 8 0 4 1 5 7 8 5 1 2 9 *